VARIOUS COLORED BETTAS

Betta splendens

The TROPICAL FISH HOBBY

By WALTER ROGERS

INCLUDING the latest in tropical fish — with the addition of color illustrations drawn from life by noted artists in the aquarium field.

IN APPRECIATION

It would have been impossible for me to write this book without the help of my former employer, Mr. Ferdinand Cochu, President of Paramount Aquarium, Inc., New York.

Mr. Cochu's many years in the tropical fish business have given him a keen insight into market conditions and what the public wants for its aquariums. He made interviews available to me with men who have traveled to the four corners of the earth, collecting the rare fish that adorn the aquarium.

It is my desire to acquaint the public with the facts about this interesting hobby. Therefore, everything possible has been included for your reading entertainment and reference.

With the hope that this book will gain friends and make many new fanciers, I dedicate it simply to the Tropical Fish Hobby.

WALTER ROGERS.

FOREWORD AND
GENERAL IDEA

THE Tropical Fish Hobby, which has been gaining in popularity for the past twenty years, now comes into its own and takes its place as one of the foremost and most educational hobbies of all.

Twenty-five years ago, when rare fish sometimes cost as much as 200 dollars each, this was a hobby exclusively for rich men. But, in the ensuing years, breeders and importers have succeeded in lowering prices to such an extent that everyone may enjoy these beautiful pets.

The aim of this book is to bring forth the latest in tropical fishes and also to instill a little of the drama, comedy and human adventure that makes this such a thrilling hobby. It is not written in a strictly scientific vein, but as a help to the beginner to better understand his fishes and their problems and to act as a guide to the more established fancier.

I have selected mostly the varieties that can be kept in the community aquarium, with the exception of "showy" fish that have individual characteristics and are seen from time to time.

THE EFFECT OF THE WAR ON THE HOBBY

In turbulent times, such as these, with so many articles off the shelves for the duration, it is not difficult to understand how the tropical fish hobby would also suffer from scarcities.

The wholesalers are doing everything possible to keep the supply of fish coming in. But, with boat space so precious and priorities so hard to get, it is a constant battle to meet the demand for new fish. As a result, the advanced fancier, realizing certain types of fish would disappear completely, applied himself to the task of selective breeding and accomplished what would have been considered impossible a few years ago. Many new fish have been developed and rare varieties bred — but unfortunately not enough to go around.

The dealers and wholesalers, therefore, urge their customers to try their hand at breeding. Certain fish are offered for that purpose. Fortunate, indeed, is the fancier who is successful. These fish bring very good prices. What could be better than to cash in on what to you was a fascinating experiment?

WHAT MAKES A FISH FANCIER?

A FUNNY question to ask, you say. Yes — but with a definite answer. Usually it is our old friend "The Guppy." People who know nothing about tropical fish have heard of Guppies. For that reason the sight of these brilliant little fellows, with the large families, pique a person's desire and as a rule start him on the road to becoming a very rabid fancier.

Then, we have the visitor to someone's home who has a well-balanced aquarium. Noticing how it adds to the surroundings and blends with the furniture of the room starts him off on that time-worn question, "How can I get an aquarium?" Which reminds me —

"*It all started with a pair of Guppies.*" The gentleman who made that statement to me has the largest breeding establishment in the South. We were standing at the door of his beautiful home, look-ing out over acres and acres of lush land dotted with ponds. At a far distance a tractor snorted and made its way from pond to pond. To my amazement, I learned that this was their method of scattering food for the fish. Truly mechanized feeding — accom-plishing in a short time what would take several men a whole day. My host explained further, some years back he had visited Florida and a friend of his had presented him with a pair of Guppies. On bringing this happy couple home, he was delighted to find not 2 Guppies but a family swimming contentedly. From that began the germ of an idea and an ambition to be fulfilled which was to make him the biggest producer of live-bearing fish in the country. Yes!!! It all started with a pair of Guppies.

COLLECTING

It has always amazed me that the collecting angle of Tropical Fish has been treated lightly or glossed over in most books. In collecting lies enough material for a complete volume and enough intrigue, mystery and hidden danger to satisfy the most hardened book fan. Rival collectors jealously guard their secrets and only their natives know in which locality the fish are found.

I have seen men return from far-off places with shipments, their bodies emaciated, skin stretched taut against their bones, burned a deep bronze, ravaged with tropical disease, but never a complaint — a month's rest and they are off again. Truly the lure of wild and unknown places have possessed these men. As a group, they are notoriously taciturn. Constant questioning, prompting and reference to certain places are the only things that made this article possible.

A large New York importer employed quite a few men in this field. As each expedition was outfitted, the Gods of Chance were the only ones who could say if it would be a success.

These men, besides being experts in their line, must also be crack marksmen, know many dialects, and have the courage to push on and on through country where no white man had ever been before. One collector related on one of his trips that he had pushed so far into the interior his natives threatened to desert him if he didn't turn back. Only cajolery and the promise of more pay saved him from an unsuccessful trip, as he was after rare species that were usually found in the virgin wilderness. Imagine this vast, empty country, where it is possible to travel several months without seeing a single human being, and then it is usually unknown tribes of Indians who have fierce habits and customs. Some are almost white, descendants of the Spaniards, who searched for the lost treasure of the Incas. Others are black as night, whose forefathers escaped from slave ships of earlier centuries. Gifts are handed out freely by the collectors to friendly and hostile tribes for obvious reasons.

Knowing the value of rare and beautiful fish, the collectors constantly search for new species and question the natives trying to locate new streams containing aquatic life. As has happened many times, a collector returning the following year may find his stream empty, denoting some other collector hit the spot before him. Sometimes the Indians poison a stream, killing all fish, to keep white men away from their locality. Often as not, the pond or stream may be dried up and lush foliage covering the spot, making it confusing to identify. Then begins the eternal hunt for more fertile territory. The hardships endured by these men are incredible.

Returning with shipments, the fish must be watched constantly, and an integral part of a collector's equipment is his gasoline compressor and tubing to provide air which is so necessary to sustain life in the fish. The stately Symphysodon discus, Pencil and Hatchet Fish must be well aerated, as they are crowded in cans, where they remain until arrival at the coastal town that serves as a transfer point to the States. This aeration is very important — No Air — No Fish!

A friend of mine, one of the youngest collectors in the business, with whom I worked for years, mentioned casually when I asked for some material, nothing much happens on his trips. By probing deep in his memory, I found several times in the last few years he miraculously escaped death and was saved once by his natives and again by a remarkable shot that blew off the head of a poisonous snake. This incident occurred as he tripped over some brush and fell a few feet from the snake. His rifle at his side, a snap shot, lucky but effective, saved him from an unpleasant demise. The dangerous Caiman (So. American Alligators) are always present and are shot quite frequently when they threaten the canoes or men.

At another place, where they made camp near a stream, they were startled to find the deadly Fer-de-lance (the most poisonous snake in So. America). These were attracted by the campfire and tried to make themselves at home among the crew. I assure you, there was a very busy few hours spent in getting rid of those unwelcome guests and not much sleep was indulged in that night.

During my last visit to New York, I made it a special point to interview Mr. Auguste Rabaut in one of his rare appearances in this country. Mr. Rabaut is, without a doubt, the Dean of Tropical Fish Collectors and has discovered many new varieties to date. His most noted discovery was the sensation of several years ago, the brilliant "Neon Tetra."

This indomitable Frenchman has been collecting and hunting since 1920. He was already an accomplished globe trotter when he became interested in tropical fish. Just before his departure one spring from Paris to hunt alligators, he met the Director of the Paris Aquarium, who asked him to bring back some tropical fish. This being a little new to him, he made it a point to learn as much as possible about them before he departed. He returned triumphantly, several months later, with approximately 5,000 fish — among them being 4 Neon Tetra. The Director, struck with the Neons' beauty, and unable to classify them, paid Rabaut 1,000 francs each (about $250.00 per fish). The Parisians being rabid tropical fish fanciers, went wild over these beauties and Rabaut, realizing the demand, started out again with Neons as the sole purpose of the trip.

The second trip was not so easy, but he managed to bring back some, along with other species. On another occasion, he brought back 8,000 specimens of one variety, only to find that there was no market for them. A dealer friend of his sold them to a neighboring country for a fraction of what he hoped to get for them. He obtained a license to fish in Brazil for the Paris Aquarium, and, after gathering a particularly large shipment, he arrived in Para and stored them in a government shed. The customs officials, surmising that some of the fish were for commercial purposes, sealed the shed and tied Rabaut up in red tape. The following 3 days were a holiday and no one would listen to his earnest entreaties concerning his fish. In desperation, he got in touch with a fellow collector, employed by a New York importer. This New York importer, knowing the importance and value of the shipment, acted at once and pulled wires, with the result that the shipment was released soon after. Mr. Rabaut came directly to the States and immediately established a connection with this importer, a connection that has proven profitable for both, but was not without the attending heartbreaks and failures. To really illustrate this point, I must relate this story as garnered through my interview with Mr. Rabaut.

On one of his return trips from So. America, in February, he was 2 days from New York after having been gone for 4½ months. He was attending a shipment that included many rare fish and 6 large electric eels. His fish were in a hold in the bow of the ship. In order to protect his charges from the cold, he had 8 specially built electric heaters and lamps placed there. A terrible storm broke and the mountainous waves, breaking over the front of the ship, prevented him from getting to where they were. The storm raged until he was almost in New York harbor. When he was finally able to investigate, he found, to his dismay, out of a shipment of 145 cans only 12 cans still contained live fish, and these, near the lamps, had survived a temperature of 48 degrees. The others died at 40 degrees. Both importers and collectors accept losses like that philosophically and always look forward to a better and more successful trip. By nature, they must be endowed with some subtle fortitude that enables them to gamble so heavily on such uncertainties as market conditions, weather, food for the fish, proper aeration, delays by officials, etc. These obstacles must always be overcome to make a successful trip.

Since the outbreak of War, Mr. Rabaut has made a trip far up the Amazon to collect fish which are impossible to breed in this country. This expedition, made more hazardous because of present conditions, meant an outlay of several thousands of dollars. The importer and Mr. Rabaut, realizing the value of shipping space in these times, made arrangements to have the fish come by plane from Barranquilla, Colombia, to Miami. This necessitated crossing unexplored country to deliver them to the shipping point. He relates that there were millions of sand flies in this region, no larger than a pinhead, but with the bite of an adult mosquito. Masks had to be worn to protect the face, and other exposed parts had to be covered with grease. This during the day. At night, savage mosquitos appeared from which there was no protection. His diet consisted of fish and more fish; no vegetables, fruit, tea or coffee. These would take up valuable space needed for his fish and supplies. After almost five months of unbelievable hardships and misadventures, he came to Barranquilla. His troubles were not over yet, as in spite of advance reservations he could not get a seat on the plane. An agent for the importer spent 5 weeks in Miami vainly waiting to receive the fish, ready for a day or night call. Mr. Rabaut finally got his shipment aboard a plane, but could not do the same for himself. The fish were crowded terribly in the relatively short hop to Miami. However, the expert care of the agent, who received them, soon had them in condition to ship by Railway Express to New York. 3,800 pounds of water were required to get them in shape for the New York trip. They arrived in New York, where the importer himself saw to it that they were given the proper care. After a journey of thousands of miles, these fish, about 30,000 of them, arrived in such good order that visitors, seeing them soon after their arrival, could not tell them apart from fish that had been there for some time. The varieties included Neon Tetra, Hatchet and Pencil Fish and 5 different kinds of Corydoras (Catfish), 1 of which is the *Corydoras rabauti*, named for this intrepid collector. Fanciers, purchasing these fish several weeks later and introducing them into their aquariums, had no idea of the story in back of the fish. In that one journey alone was material for a complete book.

An observation made by Mr. Rabaut, and which I consider quite an oddity, was during his travels in So. America, wherever there were beautiful butterflies near a stream, that stream contained beautiful fish.

Mr. Rabaut firmly believes the varieties yet to be discovered will outshine anything we now have for brilliance and beauty. And I know, in spite of the hardships involved, he will be the one to bring them out!!!

TRANSPORTING TROPICAL FISH

TRANSPORTATION has always been a major problem for the whole-sale dealer. Not only to ship fish to neighboring cities, but to bring new importations thousands of miles to this country. Few people know and realize a man must go along and watch his fish constantly during the long voyage from So. America, Singapore or some other far-off place. He must be doctor, dietitian and watchman all in one, besides having a good pair of sea-legs.

Before the War, many ocean liners had special rooms reserved for tropical fish. Men did nothing but travel back and forth and take care of each new shipment. Air lines, heating equipment and a compressor were installed and remained. Part of their job was to keep all equipment in shape. In rough weather they had to watch their charges closely, as they were liable to get seasick from the toss and roll of the ship. This meant 24-hour-a-day duty.

Several years before the War, I went to California for my health. After a few weeks, the monotony of my life began to get me, so I constructed a 20-gallon aquarium.

I wrote back East and asked if it were possible to send me some fish. A week later, to my amazement, the Express Company called and said they had some live fish for me. "Live Fish!" I couldn't understand it, as I had only inquired about the possibility of ship-ping fish. I rushed down and sure enough, there was a can, decked out with stickers saying "Live Fish," "Do not change water," "Right Side Up," etc. I took the cover off with some doubts, but there were my fish, swimming about never minding the fact they had just traveled over 3,000 miles. Not one died as a result of that trip.

Some weeks later I visited San Francisco and while there tried to obtain some rare fish, with no result. I wrote East again and this time they were sent by plane at only $1.00 a pound. All were alive and in very good shape and I mentally thanked the far-sighted pioneer who inaugurated this novel process of shipping fish.

Later that year, we met the ill-fated Zeppelin, "Hindenburg," at Lakehurst, N. J., and received a shipment of tropical fish from Europe. After inspection, we rushed them to Newark Airport, where we put them on a plane for Chicago, beating all records in shipping live stock. By the time they reached their destination, they had traveled over 5,500 miles in only 60 hours. They made "headline" news and remained on exhibition in the Shedd Aquarium.

Mr. Walter H. Chute, Director of the Shedd Aquarium, Chicago, and a famous collector of tropical fish, explained to me quite recently that before any extensive shipping of fish can be done by air, a method must be perfected whereby the shipping cans can be properly insulated to protect the fish against the terrific cold of the stratosphere.

Mr. Chute, recognized by many as one of the foremost aquarists in the country, has solved many difficult transportation problems connected with fish. Since the Shedd Aquarium is inland, salt water is not always available, but on display there in Chicago will be found many beautiful and delicate inhabitants of tropical seas. Fish, Mr. Chute traveled thousands of miles to collect and bring home, now occupy well set-up tanks that make them feel right at home. The citizens of Chicago can well be proud of their beautiful aquarium, stocked with so many rare fish that heretofore have been unknown so far inland.

AQUARIUM SOCIETIES

In most large cities and towns there are groups of fanciers banded together to form an Aquarium Society. The purpose of these societies is to bring together the tropical fish fanciers — both beginner and expert — for a mutual exchange of ideas and happenings in the tanks of their owners.

There, one can hear talks by interesting people on numerous subjects that have a direct connection with the home aquarium and also any of the minor problems that arise from time to time. Too much cannot be said for these societies, as the people who belong are sincere persons who want to learn all they can of their hobby and also pass along any information they may have obtained from other sources. Quite often fish are exchanged or a prize of a pair of rare fish may be offered for one reason or another. Find out where the one nearest you is located and when they meet. I feel certain you will attend every meeting and profit by the knowledge you obtain. There is also a good monthly magazine, "The Aquarium," on the market. This magazine contains valuable articles and is widely circulated.

MANAGEMENT OF THE AQUARIUM

SIZE

In selecting your aquarium, the size and quality are important factors. A better type aquarium is cheaper in the long run, as it is to be your fishes' home for a long time. Sizes range from one to 100 gallons. Since a 1-gallon tank holds only 5 fishes at the most, a 10-gallon is considered the most appropriate size for the beginner, for it will comfortably hold 10 pair of average size fish.

AQUARIUM ON STAND

LOCATION AND LIGHT

THE best location for your aquarium is in front of or close to a window, where the sun will shine on it for at least a few hours daily. Sunlight is beneficial, although not necessary, if you have electrically lighted hoods or top reflectors. Without sunlight, several hours of artificial light are needed daily to stimulate plant growth and keep the aquarium balanced.

Since this is the latest book on the market, we must mention the latest advance made in aquarium lighting. The fluorescent light has invaded the aquarium field with amazing results. For plant growth and reflecting the beauty of your fish, it is a revelation. This long bulb (equipped with a transformer that cuts the light bill in half) throws a soft blue-white light to every corner of the aquarium, causing the plants to grow vigorously and the fish to reflect opalescent tints that are a joy to behold.

PROPER NATURAL LIGHT

ARTIFICIAL LIGHT

The John G. Shedd Aquarium of Chicago has had all their tropical fish tanks equipped with fluorescent lights. The comments of an admiring public have proven what an innovation was made in aquarium lighting.

PROPER HEAT FOR THE AQUARIUM

THE temperature in the aquarium should be kept between 74 and 78 degrees if possible. A fluctuation of a few degrees is not harmful. It is more a question of getting your fish used to your particular room temperature. What must be avoided at all times is a sudden drop, as from 74 to 60 degrees, in a short space of time. This will cause trouble.

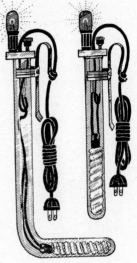

Take precautions to see that it does not happen. While the temperature may be suitable during the day, at night the room may become cool. As room temperature affects the aquarium water, the larger the aquarium the less rapid the fluctuations. A point in favor of a larger aquarium.

To alleviate the mind, there are quite a few good heaters on the market. A reliable unit equipped with automatic control will insure an even temperature at all times. The steady way it reacts to sudden changes in room temperature reminds one of a silent sentinel always on duty. Remember, a good heater and thermostat, though a little more expensive, can be depended upon, whereas a cheap heater cannot. Since your collection of fish will be worth many times what your heater cost, this is indeed an insurance worth taking.

AQUARIUM HEATER

PLANTS

BEFORE listing the different plants available, perhaps it would be wise to mention that just as the garden needs careful planning, so does the aquarium. To show all plants to their best advantage, use any method desired, but keep in mind that attractiveness must be the keynote and harmonious blending of the plants you use will produce a startling and satisfying effect.

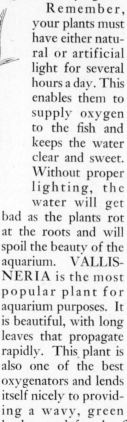

Remember, your plants must have either natural or artificial light for several hours a day. This enables them to supply oxygen to the fish and keeps the water clear and sweet. Without proper lighting, the water will get bad as the plants rot at the roots and will spoil the beauty of the aquarium. VALLISNERIA is the most popular plant for aquarium purposes. It is beautiful, with long leaves that propagate rapidly. This plant is also one of the best oxygenators and lends itself nicely to providing a wavy, green background for the fish. The number of these plants are dependent upon the size of the aquarium. SAGITTARIA is somewhat like Vallisneria in general appearance, but is available in various sizes (3 or 4 varieties are usually to be had) and is a bit

GIANT SAGITTARIA
(*Sagittaria sinensis*)

VALLISNERIA
(*Vallisneria spiralis*)

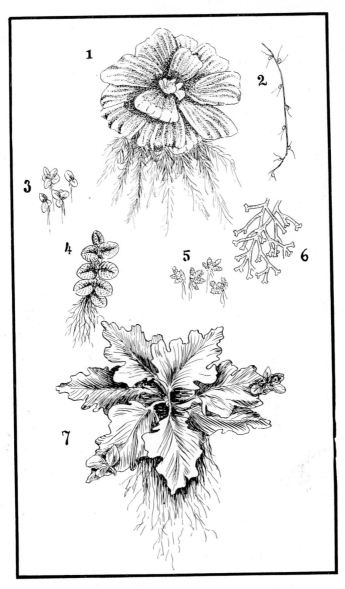

1—Water Lettuce   5—Azolla
2—Urticularia Minor   6—Riccia
3—Duckweed   7—Water Fern
4—Salvinia

heavier in leaf structure. The most suitable size for background work is SAGITTARIA NATANS. This plant is about 8 or 9 inches high. The GIANT SAGITTARIA, a large bushy plant, is a "stand out" wherever placed. DWARF VARIETIES, tiny 4- or 5-stemmed plants, form an attractive carpet around large plants or rockwork in the aquarium.

ANACHARIS – Bushy, hardy and very prolific. It is a handy refuge for baby fish. Each bit is the bud end of a stem 6 to 8 inches long and has a whorl of dark green leaves along the entire stem. The stems should be planted separately but grouped together for best effects. They soon develop roots. Since Anacharis grows rapidly, it must be cut occasionally. Merely snip off the ends and dispose of the clippings much like trimming a garden hedge.

Other favorable plants include (see illustration) LUDWIGIA, CRYPTOCORYNE, SPATTERDOCK, CABOMBA, HAIR GRASS and the SO. AMERICAN SWORD PLANT, a very beautiful, decorative plant, excellent as a centerpiece. Grows long leaves and is especially desirable in a large, deep aquarium. They are being raised in this country and can be had from time to time. There are

Sagittaria natans

ANACHARIS

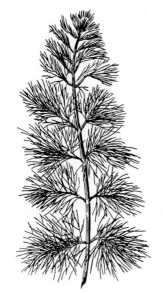

CABOMBA
(Cabomba caroliniana)

LUDWIGIA
(Ludwigia mullerti)

NARROW CRYPTOCORYNE
(Crytocoryne willisii)

SPATTERDOCK
(Nuphar sagittoefolia)

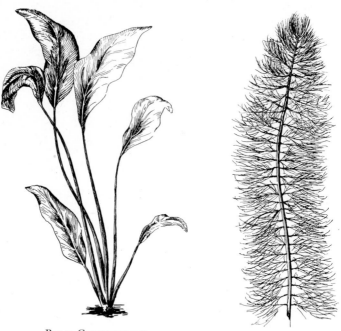

Broad Cryptocoryne
(*Crytocoryne griffithii*)

Myriophyllum

Lace Plant

broad and narrow-leaf varieties. Both lend added attractiveness to the aquarium. A very rare plant that is seldom seen is the striking MADAGASCAR LACE PLANT, an excellent centerpiece that adds rare beauty to the aquarium and at one time sold at fantastic prices. This list will give you an idea as to the number of plants usually available for aquarium purposes. They are decorative and lend themselves ideally to aquascaping.

For breeding, recommended plants are MYRIOPHYLLUM, RICCIA, UTRICULARIA and NITELLA. These provide a safe hiding place for baby fish and an ideal place for egg-laying fish to deposit their eggs.

ROCKS AND ORNAMENTS

THERE are quite a few natural rocks that can be found which will blend with your tank arrangement. These can be placed in various parts of the tank, half hidden by sand. Will form convenient hiding places for small fish and at the same time look like a natural bottom of a brook or lake to carry out the illusion of the perfect home for your fish. There are other ornaments, such as divers, sunken ships, treasure chests, etc. One must suit his own particular taste in this matter. Always strive for an artistic setting that looks natural.

GRAVEL

THIS is an inexpensive item and you have your choice of various colors. A 10-gallon standard size tank would need about 20 pounds, figuring 2 pounds to a gallon. This may seem like a lot, but you must have enough to enable your plants to take root and also to do your aquascaping.

Have it slope towards the front of the tank, as this enables you to keep it clean with very little effort, as the débris gathers in front and can be syphoned easily. Never use beach sand. It is impractical, as it must be cured and treated before it can be used in the aquarium. In view of the low cost of purchasable aquarium sand, it is not worth the trouble.

Rinse gravel thoroughly before using, because it picks up dust en route. Although unwashed gravel is not harmful, it may cause the tank to become cloudy for awhile. The best way to do this is to place gravel in a pot or can. Hold container under the faucet and permit water to flow into it. Keep stirring gravel with your hand until the water is absolutely clear. This will take a little extra energy on your part, but we feel sure you will be delighted with the crystal-clear aquarium you will have as a result.

SETTING UP THE AQUARIUM

BEFORE introducing plants, have the aquarium half full of water. This is easier than trying to arrange plants with a full tank. Pour the water in carefully, arrange gravel high in back with a slope to the front and planting may begin.

In planting, care should be taken to do it right. You thus avoid having plants come up or choked as a result of improper handling. In arranging plants, the taller Vallisneria shows best at the rear of the tank, half an inch apart (a handy tool for planting is the aquarium tong—see illustration under accessories). Grasp the root of the plant with thumb and index finger and push gently into the sand. Then go on to the next. Be careful not to plant too deeply. Use caution not to bury the crown of the plant. Runners, from which new plants develop, grow from the crown and usually extend toward the light, along the gravel surface.

The Sagittaria is planted like Vallisneria, the root being covered with gravel, arranged in groups of 3 or 4 just in front of the Vallisneria. The shorter, more robust Sagittaria appears to good advantage.

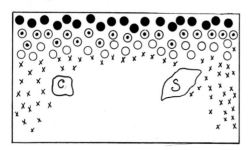

PLANTING ARRANGEMENTS

Solid Spot—Vallisneria
Circle and Spot—Sagittaria sinensis
Circle—Sagittaria subulatta

X—Hairgrass
C—Spatterdock
S—Stone

Anacharis should be planted in a clump or group. Try for a natural effect in arranging and leave front of aquarium clear. You may have a rock ornament. If so, put plants in back or on one side to achieve the desired effect and balance. Use any plants that suit your fancy, but do not try for too much variety unless a very large aquarium is used. Do not overcrowd aquarium with plants, as they must have room for developing and the fish must have enough space for exercise.

INTRODUCTION OF FISH

WHEN aquarium is fully planted and arranged, cover water surface with a sheet of paper before filling. This will prevent plants from coming loose and gravel being disturbed. Fill to upper frame, as the aquarium is most attractive when filled to capacity. A newly planted tank should stand for at least 3 days before fish are introduced. It is well, during this period, to leave the light on as much as possible so that plants may take root and the water adjust itself to the proper temperature for receiving fish.

It is inadvisable to begin with a large collection of fish. Only put in a few pairs at the start and wait a couple of days before getting more.

Do not feed the new fish for at least 24 hours. This gives them an opportunity to become acquainted in the new environment. The pleasure you derive from a well-balanced aquarium is unequalled and more than makes up for the time and effort you put into arriving at this desired goal.

To keep your aquarium in the peak of condition, it is necessary to add water from time to time to make up for evaporation. This acts for the fish the same way it would for us when we open our windows for fresh air. Also syphon out any sediment or unconsumed food that may be on the bottom of the aquarium. Aquariums have stayed crystal clear for years as a result of simple methods such as these.

FOOD AND FEEDING

FOOD and feeding are important. This is an obvious fact. Whenever possible, give your fish live food. The different types listed here are somewhat seasonable, as your dealer must take what is available to him during the year. DAPHNIA, or Water Fleas, as they are sometimes called, are available from Spring to late Fall and are considered the most popular of live foods. There is also MOSQUITO LARVAE at the pet shops for a short time during the summer. This is taken very readily by most fish. During the cold season a variety is offered that includes TUBIFEX, GLASS LARVAE, WHITE WORMS and CYCLOPS. A small portion of these foods do not cost much and will last for several days, depending on the amount of fish you have. Your dealer will gladly give you any information on live food and which type your particular fish would enjoy.

The prepared dried foods, that are staples for the fish, come in three sizes, FINE, MEDIUM and COARSE. The MEDIUM is best for the average size fish, but where you have baby fish the FINER food is needed, and for large fish, COARSE. Good alternates are DRIED SHRIMP and FLAKE FOOD.

1-1a. Mosquita larva   4. Daphnia
2. Cyclops   5. Cypris
3-3a. Hydra   6. Blood worm
          7. Tubifex

In the beginning, care must be exercised in feeding your fish. It is better to underfeed than to overfeed. Experiment by dropping a

WORM FEEDERS

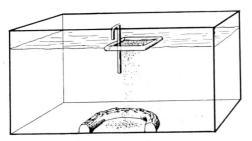

FOOD RING AND RESERVOIR IN USE IN AQUARIUM

little in the tank and watch them eat it up. Follow with a little more. Keep this up until they lose interest. Then STOP! By doing this for a few days, the proper amount required may be judged. Too much food in the aquarium settles to the bottom and will decompose and pollute the water, causing your fish to die. One feeding a day is the proper procedure to follow. Rotate your food so each feeding is different. If you leave home for a day or two, please do not have a friend or neighbor feed your fish. It can be disastrous to allow one who is not familiar with fish the task of feeding them. Fish will not suffer if they are not fed for a day or two.

INFUSORIA, whether collected or cultivated, is a necessary food for baby fish not large enough to take daphnia. Cultivation is comparatively easy, usually accomplished by putting lettuce or spinach in a small tank with several snails. Allow greens to decay. The snails eat the greens in this state and their droppings result in the development of Infusoria. Certain breeders have their own methods, but most greens, in a decomposed state, will produce some type of infusoria.

BRINE SHRIMP is another popular food for baby fish. This is slightly smaller than young daphnia and comes in dry form, packaged with full directions. Following these will provide a healthy live food for the young fry.

ACCESSORIES

AN aquarium, once established, is little trouble and requires a minimum of care. However, the discriminating aquarist will probably avail him or herself of some of the practical tools on the market. These include THERMOMETER, DIP TUBE, NET, FOOD RING and SCRAPER. Others often used are the WORM FEEDER, PLANTING TONGS and BREEDING TRAP. A breeding trap (see illustration under live-bearers) is very handy for the fancier who desires to breed

and cross-breed live-bearing fish. This trap fits into breeding tank
and female is placed in it. (A good idea is to do this several days
before young are expected, as it is not advisable to move the female
when she is too heavy.) The ingenious arrangement of the trap
permits the young, when born, to swim out between sides or
bottom, thus saving them from being eaten by the mother fish.
She cannot follow because of her size. When the dip tube is placed
in the tank, the bulb rapidly fills with water, draining with it the
objectionable matter. This is a cheap accessory that is quite
necessary.

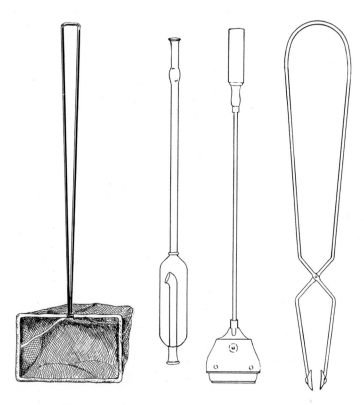

NET   DIP TUBE, SCRAPER AND TONGS

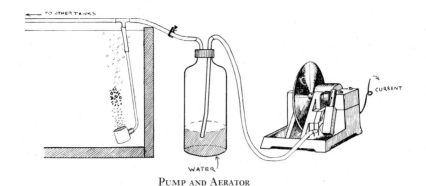

PUMP AND AERATOR

AERATION

In home aquariums, that are two well stocked with fish, the aquarist will notice the fish swimming near the top. This sign points to the fact that the oxygen is being exhausted faster than plants can replace it. To remedy this, you must have a larger aquarium, less fish, or an AERATOR. This especially constructed air pump provides the oxygen the plants lack and makes it possible to have several times the normal amount of fish in the aquarium. The average dealer uses AERATION. This means he has an air pump that supplies air through a rubber hose with a porous stone at the end. If you have an AERATOR you are at once in a position to avail yourself of the boon of the aquarist, namely, a FILTER. This filter (there

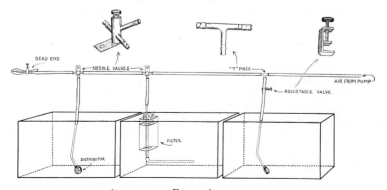

AERATOR AND FILTER ARRANGEMENT

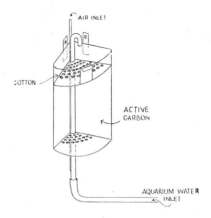

INSIDE FILTER

are several types — inside and outside) is a deep boxlike affair with a layer of pebbles in the bottom, next a layer of carbon and on top clean cotton or sand. It filters the aquarium water constantly and keeps it sweet and pure and also lessens time ordinarily spent in cleaning the aquarium.

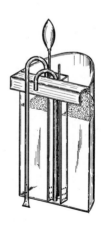

OUTSIDE FILTER

ENEMIES

THE use of live food and wild plants makes it possible to introduce an enemy occasionally. Of course, conscientious dealers do everything in their power to prevent such an occurrence. But, just in case, we are listing most types in order that you may recognize them if found in the aquarium and net them out with all possible haste.

The most common enemy found in the aquarium is HYDRA, a fresh-water polyp (see illustration under Feeding), This tiny octopuslike creature delights in snaring baby fish for his meals. Others include, as per illustration:

1. Diving Beetle Larva
2. Damsel Fly Larva
3. Diving Bettle
4. Water Tiger
5. Caddis Worm
6. Water Scorpion

HOSPITAL OR QUARANTINE TANK

BEFORE mentioning fish diseases and how to treat them, we suggest a valuable hint to aid in the proper treatment and lessen the possibility of having contagion spread throughout the aquarium. A smaller tank or container should be kept near your large home aquarium. This would serve the purpose of a hospital. Any fish suspected of being sick could be dispatched to it and placed under observation until all was well. Of course, in cases of "ICH," which is discussed in a succeeding paragraph, you must cure the whole tank. However, this additional tank may save an entire valuable collection for its owner. Make sure temperatures are the same in both tanks.

DISEASES

IF one has a healthy tank, where the plants are growing nicely and the temperature is controlled, they will rarely have any trouble with sick fish. However, a sick fish may be introduced or a sudden drop in temperature may cause trouble. This list, therefore, will include most of the ills fish are subject to and enable you to recognize and treat accordingly.

ICH *(Ichthophthirius)* is a parasite present in almost all aquariums. A sudden chill may weaken a fish and lower its resistance, thus making it more susceptible to this disease. SYMPTOMS: Tiny white spots appear on body, tail or fins. Fish will become less active, begin to wiggle and scrape along the bottom over gravel and stones. Fins are held close to the body and the tail is pinched. TREATMENT: Gradually raise temperature to 85 degrees. Dissolve

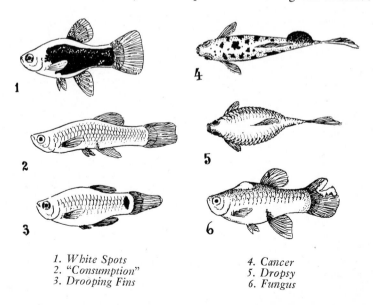

1. *White Spots*
2. *"Consumption"*
3. *Drooping Fins*

4. *Cancer*
5. *Dropsy*
6. *Fungus*

a tablespoonful of sea salt to each gallon of water in which the fish are placed. Do not feed during this period. Purchase one of the several good preparations on the market and use as advised.*

FUNGUS is an infection caused by an injury. This may happen by the fish jumping out of the tank and injuring its protective slime tissue. Or perhaps a larger, unfriendly fish may inflict a slight wound. Other causes are fish being scared and dashing into the side of the tank, bruising head or mouth. SYMPTOMS: Small cottonlike or darker sorelike blotches on the body of the fish. This will spread over the entire body if not checked and prove fatal to the fish. If a grayish white film appears around the lips, that is white mouth or mouth fungus. TREATMENT: There are several remedies available for the treatment of fungus. Follow the manufacturer's directions.†

THIN AND SUNKEN BODIES is commonly called CONSUMPTION. SYMPTOMS: Hollow or shrunken bodies. This is due to old age or poor aquarium conditions. Fish in this state are pretty far gone. You may test your ingenuity in curing it by placing it alone in your hospital tank and tempting it with choice morsels such as Daphnia or Worms. This has been known to produce results in some cases.

TAIL OR FIN ROT. This condition, like fungus, is from an injury or a bite from another fish. Sometimes, where the aquarium water is highly acid, fish will exhibit the following SYMPTOMS: As the name implies, this disease attacks and rots away the tail and fins. They become frayed and usually show a grayish white substance around the edges. TREATMENT: In mild cases, fish do not have to be removed. Use Fungus Remedy as prescribed. In severe cases, remove fish and treat alone.

To test water for acid condition or for breeding purposes, it is well to have a TESTING KIT on hand. This handy kit can change the water from alkaline to acid by the application of certain chemicals contained therein and shows you how to obtain correct pH of your aquarium water. The color chart, that is included, makes all tests simple and no technical knowledge is necessary.

---

* A good first-aid treatment, until a good preparation can be purchased, is to use 2 drops of 2% Mercurochrome to every gallon of water.

† Salt may be used as a first-aid treatment. Dissolve one teaspoonful to each gallon of water.

ALGAE

ALGAE is usually the result of too much light. There are several types of algae, but the one most often encountered is the common Green Algae. This forms on the glass and detracts from the beauty of the aquarium. However, the water remains clear and certain fish relish it as an added delicacy. The Kissing Gouramies, Mollies and Swordtails attack it immediately. Therefore, do not be in a rush to remove it as the fish may do the job for you.

Another type Algae is a very heavy, brownish color. Once entrenched in the tank, it is very hard to remove. Even snails pass this by and to date the only fish who will attempt to eat it is the Kissing Gourami. To remove, the best implement on the market is the AQUARIUM SCRAPPER. This species of Algae propagates rapidly and should be removed quickly and thoroughly or it will occur again in several days.

SNAILS

SNAILS are good scavengers in the aquarium and for this reason most tanks have one or two. They eat some of the excess food on the bottom and keep the glass sides of the aquarium free of algae to the best of their ability. Since they are known as plant eaters, it is not wise to put them in an aquarium with delicate, expensive plants. The only snail that will not touch plants is the *Ampullaria cuprina* or MYSTERY SNAIL, very popular for this reason and also because it is an excellent scavenger. Other types include the RED RAMSHORN, COLOMBIAN RAMSHORN, AUSTRALIAN RED, AFRICAN PAPER SHELL and the COMMON POND SNAIL, that propagates rapidly. All species are hardy and spawn in the tank. However, fish will eat spawn unless measures are taken to prevent them.

1—Four Horned
2—Australian Red
3—Columbian
4—Trumpet

5—Red Ramshorn
6—Japanese
7—Common Pond
8—African Paper Shell

IDENTIFICATION OF FINS

THROUGHOUT this book will be found references to certain fins and their names. It is well for the fancier to acquaint himself with these fins and their location on the fish. This will help immeasurably in identifying the various families displayed in community aquariums. The illustration gives a clear picture of all fins:

Spinous — Spinous.

D — Dorsal fin.

D2 — Soft dorsal.

AD — Adipose, common in the Characin group.

C — Caudal, the tail fin.

G — Gill cover.

P — Pectoral fins.

V — Ventral fins.

AN — Anal fins.

S — Scales.

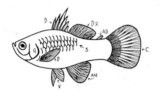

FIN FORMATION

LIVE BEARERS

THESE fish are just what the name implies, a hardy, prolific family that has done more to delight fanciers than all other fish combined. The genuine pleasure derived by the beginner, who sees live babies

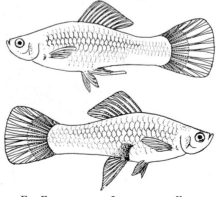

FIN FORMATION OF LIVE-BEARING FISH

being born before his eyes, is one of the factors that makes him become a loyal and resolute devotee of the hobby from that time on. How he nurses those tiny babies and lavishes care with an open hand!

The more advanced aquarist finds these fish ideal for cross-breeding to bring out new colors. By crossing Platies and Helleries, he develops new Hybrids. For breeding, always make sure that the female is strong, full bellied and rounded. In listing this family, we will group some together in order to list as many as possible. This will make your selection both wide and varied.

Most of these fish prefer dried food to live and are easy to please in this matter. If you have a full female, and you can recognize this by the large black spot at the bottom of the belly, put her in a separate aquarium with a good deal of Nitella. This is for the babies to hide in. All fish, with the exception of the Mollies, may eat their babies. If you have a BREEDING TRAP, all the better. Place the female inside and as babies are born they swim out between the glass, free from harm.

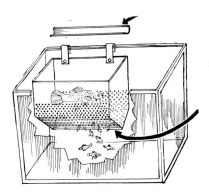

COMBINATION BREEDING TRAP
AND NURSERY TANK

LEBISTES RETICULATUS

GUPPY

THIS fish, known to almost everyone, will breed anywhere, even under difficult conditions. It stands temperatures from 60 degrees to 100, is active, stands close confinement, foul water and, while not a fighter, is not timid. As in most tropical fish, the males are the more beautiful. They are extremely variable. Of all the millions sold, there have probably never been 2 alike. The females are much less brilliant, a rather drab olive with a green iridescence. They grow to a length of 2½ inches, while the males seldom exceed one inch.

They are found in Guiana, Venezuela, Trinidad and parts of Mexico. The fertility of the fish has made it ideal for cross-breeding, and the fanciers and breeders have developed such variations as GOLD, SWORD TAIL (long spear on tail), BLACK TAIL (long flowing jet black tail), and the latest, which I saw at a fancier's house who developed the fish, THE VICTORY GUPPY, so named because of the perfect V in the tail, almost as long as the body.

Fanciers always look for large dorsals, colorful markings and

Lebistes reticulatus

characteristics which may produce something new in a Guppy. THE TRINIDAD GUPPY was found in the same locality as the ordinary Guppy by a fancier on vacation. He was amazed to find most males were alike, a bronze gold color. And this is unusual — the females had color, too, gold with bluish color in tail and fins.

GOLD WAGTAIL PLATY   RED WAGTAIL PLATY

Red Platy
Old Red Platy
Gold Crescent Platy   Black Platy
Red Crescent Platy   Gold Platy

PLATYPOECILUS MACULATUS

PLATIES OR MOON FISH

THESE live bearers, when originally found in So. Mexico, were dirty, grayish fish, mottled and splotched. The wide variety of colors offered today show the result of careful breeding. They are graceful, showy fish and come in BLACK, BLUE, GREEN, GOLD and RED. The RED PLATY has a deep red color that took years to develop. There are many hybrids of this species that have had a remarkable blending of colors, but the solid color PLATIES seem to be the most popular with the fanciers. The name *Platypoecilia* means "broad bodied" and *Maculatus* means "spotted." The males are about 1½ inches and the females 2 inches. Another standout variation is the GOLD HELMET BLACK PLATY. This is a shimmering black fish with a gold crown. Dr. Myron Gordon, of the New York Zoological Society, produced one of the latest variations to date by crossing a wild "COMET" PLATY to a domesticated GOLDEN one. By repeating this and selecting young with individual markings, the result was the RED and GOLD WAGTAIL PLATY. This fish is red with black fins and golden sheen on body. Truly a distinctive-looking fish and a tribute to the patience of the men who are constantly trying for new variations. The *Platy variatus* created a sensation here on its arrival from Mexico some years ago. The name *Variatus* means "varied" and it is indeed varied in color. Variations range from ORANGE to BLACK with BLUE SPOTS and RED TAILS. Same length as the MACULATUS, but, strangely enough, in this fish the males are as large as the females, but can easily be distinguished by the pointed anal on the male. Outstanding variations occur here. Truly a fish worth having. It is hardy and for short periods can stand a temperature as low as 50 degrees. Very prolific.

XIPHOPHORUS HELLERI

SWORDTAIL OR HELLERI

EASTERN Mexico was the original habitat of this fish. It has a striking appearance and lively ways that delight the aquarist. The original stock sold at the then fancy price of 10 dollars a pair. They were strongly overcast with iridescent green and had metallic green in the tail spike. The saw-tooth line, along the center of the body, was red and distinctly formed. The tail sword in the male was straight and long. Being good breeders, they lent themselves nicely to selective breeding with many variations. Chief among which is the RED SWORDTAIL. This fish is considered a Hybrid developed, so the story goes, as a result of the mating between a male Red Platy and a female Swordtail. Be that as it may, the fish is extremely beautiful. The deep red body has a white chest and the sword is gold with black edging.

Other hybrids and variations are the MONTEZUMAE HELLERI. In general color, this fish is a warm yellowish red with brown to black markings. It is quite fertile and grows, in some cases, to a length of 4½ inches exclusive of the sword. Others are RUBRA or BERLIN HELLERI, GOLD and RED ALBINO HELLERI, BLACK HELLERI, GOLD HELLERI and the latest produced so far, the BLACK TUXEDO HELLERI, so named because of markings that resemble a tuxedo, white chest with a broad black band around the sides and blue-green coloring on top. This has also been produced in RED and is called the RED TUXEDO HELLERI. Most male hybrids have very short swords and some males have none at all. Breeding requires several healthy females and plenty of plants for young to hide in.

Old Red Helleri
Black Helleri
New Red Helleri
Orange Helleri
Gold Helleri

MOLLIENISIA

MOLLIE

THIS gentle fish, next to our friend the Guppy, deserves the title of the "most popular aquarium fish." They are natives of our own country, frequenting the brackish water streams of Florida and North Carolina. They are very prolific, having young at intervals of 30 days or so. A batch consists of from 40 to 50. These mature very slowly in home aquariums, but grow beautifully in outdoor pools. The MOLLIE likes algae and a tank that has plenty will provide an ideal home for the fish.

MOLLIENISIA LATIPINNA

SAILFIN MOLLIE

LATIPINNA, meaning "broad-fin," does not exaggerate the hand-some Sailfin. When displayed in its motions courting the female, it is an unforgettable sight. These fish are quite large and need to be kept in a large tank. The male's dorsal fin is a light blue with pearl dots, tail blue with yellow flecks and body olive with blue and green stripes. Black Mollies are the most common for aqua-rium use. The original color was a grayish black. But again, selective breeding produced a strain JET BLACK, BORN BLACK and STAY BLACK. There is a larger Black Mollie, produced from very selected stock. This is the "show fish" of the Mollie family and wins prizes wherever shown. It is known as the BLACK SAILFIN MOLLIE. It is deep, midnight black with gold eyes, and the male has a huge sailfin, black with an orange border. Other Mollies include the SPHENOPS, very colorful. Most of them are beautifully marked, and, while they lack the large dorsal fin of the other Mollies, they more than make up for it in attractive markings. The male has a striking orange-fringed tail, body color black flecked with blue. A variety of the *Sphenops* is the LIBERTY MOLLIE, a large active fish that attains 4 inches. The female has almost no color except for a steel blue body. The male makes up for this, however, by a distinctive dorsal of red, white and blue. The body is steel blue, tail red and black.

Mollienisia velifera Female   *Mollienisia velifera* Male
                                       Mollienisia latipunctata Male

Mollienisia latipinna Male   Black Sailfin Mollie Male
          Black Mollie Male

LIMIA VITTATA

BLUE LIMIA

WHILE there are quite a few Limias on the market, we are only listing 2 most often seen and easiest to care for. The *Limia vittata*, because of its extreme fertility (this fish set the all-time record for its kind at the Shedd Aquarium, Chicago, giving birth to 242 babies). Easy to breed, best temperature about 75 degrees. Color is not bright, but delicately shaded, greenish brown body with blue flecks running through the middle; in some specimens dark, irregular lines are to be found on the body. Dorsal and tail fins pale yellow. Easy to distinguish the male by the pointed anal fin of the live bearer.

LIMIA NIGROFASCIATA

HUMP-BACKED LIMIA

As the male of this species begins to age, its back forms a sort of hump. This does not detract from its appearance, however, as the dorsal increases in size and makes it very attractive when it courts the female. This fish, like the *Vittata*, is an energetic breeder and has been crossed with other Limias to form some very interesting hybrids. The color is a transparent gray with dark bars. (In older fish the body color is light gold with bars.) Has young from 5 to 6 weeks after fertilization. These are hardy and while not numerous (about 25 in a batch) mature rapidly, if kept in spacious surroundings, with algae to feed on. Temperature, 75 degrees. The Limias are to be found in Cuba and Haiti.

Limia nigrofasciata Male
Limia vittata Male   *Limia nigrofasciata* Female
Limia vittata Female
Limia heterandria Male
Limia heterandria Female
Limia caudofasciata Male
Limia caudofasciata Female

LABYRINTH FISH

BUBBLE NEST BUILDERS

THIS species, so called because of its curious breathing habits, is interesting not only for its brilliant colors, but also for the fascination it provides at breeding time. There are scientific books that describe this process in minute detail. We will only attempt to cover the important points for your edification. These fish, and the male does most of the work, put on a spectacular display. For your identification, when it is ready to breed, it very painstakingly builds a nest of bubbles on top, in a corner of the aquarium or near floating plants. Because of the gill structure of the fish, it breathes underwater and also above. When the nest is finished, place a strong healthy female in the aquarium and watch the fun begin. The male, an ardent swain, treats the female pretty rough and in some cases injures her. The actual mating occurs when he wraps himself around her completely and squeezes the eggs from her. As they sink down through the water he immediately fertilizes them. He then catches them in his mouth and deposits them in the nest. This goes on for some time until several hundred eggs are handled thusly. These hatch in about 48 hours. The female should be removed when mating is through. Father does all the work from here on and watches his babies with tender solicitude. When young fish appear, a culture of infusoria (discussed under feeding) should be handy to start them on the diet so necessary for baby fish.

The male is at its best during this breeding period. Its colors flame intensely and highlights are noticed that often escape attention. For an intimate view of the fishes love-life, the mating and breeding of the LABYRINTH FISH has no parallel. For most successful results, keep temperature around 80 degrees.

MACROPODUS VIRIDI AURATUS
RED PARADISE

THIS is one of the oldest of aquarium fish, known and used in Europe back in the 19th century and brought to this country about 1876. These hardy fish survive temperatures of 50 degrees and at one time lived with goldfish. However, frayed tails and numerous wounds on the goldfish bespoke this fish's antagonistic nature. For a time it was kept only with fish of its own kind. However, its beautiful color and flowing fins kept up its popularity and it is now seen in many aquariums with larger fish.

It breeds easily (Bubble Nest as described). Is greenish brown with blue-green and red stripes. The fins are partially red with blue stripes on border, dark spots on back. Female is paler, with smaller fins. Grows to 3 inches.

MACROPODUS
WHITE OR ALBINO PARADISE

THERE seems to be some doubt as to where this fish originated or developed. The most logical, and to my mind, the correct classification is that they are sports from the Red Paradise, seized by an alert breeder and gradually by selective breeding developed into the fish we have today. They were considered quite a novelty when introduced in this country from Germany in 1933. They breed true and have a very peaceful nature. They have the pink eyes of the true albino, faint bars ranging from pink to red, body white or cream colored. Easy and prolific breeders.

MACROPODUS CUPANUS DAYI
DWARF PARADISE

THIS fish, while slightly smaller than the other Paradise Fish, has a good name among aquarists. Hardy, tame and prolific, it adds to any community tank. Body brown with green glitter, 2 dark lines through body and red fins. Breeds as described. Like the other Paradise Fish (and this is quite a feature) it is long-lived, eats anything served and survives even foul water. These fish average in size from 1½ to 2 inches.

Female *Macropodus opercularis*
Male *Macropodus opercularis*
White Paradise
Macropodus cupanus dayi

COLISA LALIA

DWARF GOURAMI

THE male in this species is an outstanding example of blended color. A rather timid fish that learns from association with other fish not to hide his beauty behind plants. The best description that would do justice to him is that his colors are like precious stones set in predominating red and blue. His body glitters as he makes his cautious way around the tank. His feelers are orange-red. The female is quite pale in comparison.

Easy and interesting to breed. Average size, 2 inches.

COLISA FASCIATA

GIANT OR STRIPED GOURAMI

THIS big fellow grows up to 5 inches and is usually kept with large fish in big aquariums. The name *Fasciata*, meaning stripes or bands, gave him the common title used above. These stripes are a deep blue on a reddish background, tail red, mouth and fins pale red. As in most Gouramis, this species originally came from India. Has large batches that grow rapidly.

TRICHOGASTER PECTORALIS

SNAKESKIN GOURAMI

THIS hardy fish is eclipsed by its relatives for showiness, but its peaceful nature, and the obliging way it has large spawns, keep it very much in the aquarium picture. A series of dark brown spots through its middle and light gold bars on an olive background complete its color scheme. The male has an amber cast to his anal fin and a long dorsal that is slightly pointed toward the back.

TRICHOGASTER SUMATRANUS
BLUE GOURAMI

This is now the most common of the GOURAMIS and most often seen in aquariums. The prolific nature of this fish caused it to be bred in such quantities that the price was cut to a great extent. It replaced the old 3-spot Gourami now seldom seen and adds solid color to any group. Eats anything and is very hardy. Its body is light blue-green, with 2 black spots in the center. Has thick lips and grows to 5 inches. Average size, 2 inches.

TRICHOGASTER LEERI
GOURAMI

This is an aristocratic-looking fish, gentle and ideal for community life. The male, in breeding season, has a scarlet chest that seems to flame against his light green body. Bluish, pearly dots are scattered throughout this color scheme and a jagged black line runs from his mouth through the eye and fades out near the tail. Fins are colorful and lacy with black dots.

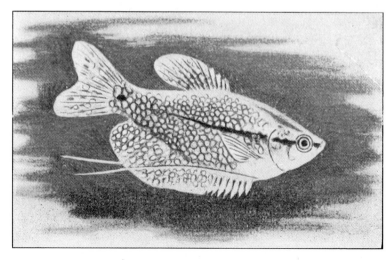

Trichogaster leeri

Colisa fasciata
Trichogaster sumatranus
Colisa lalia
Colisa labiosa

HELOSTOMA TEMMINCKI

KISSING GOURAMI

This Gourami, with the peculiar name, makes the best copy of all Gouramis. Its features are legion and few community tanks are without a pair. Besides their interesting habits, they perform valuable service for their owners.

They have wide protractile lips that are constantly in motion. They place these lips on the glass sides of the aquarium and go up and down all over the tank. This keeps the aquarium free of too much algae which can mar its appearance. The type of algae does not bother this fish. It takes them all in stride. It goes up and down the plants in this same manner, cleaning all the time. The most delicate plants have never been harmed by this treatment, but seem to thrive as a result. A pair in the tank will sometimes meet and in a slight shift here and there you are treated to the sight of two fishes KISSING — and what a kiss! Mouths locked together, they remain motionless for as long as 15 minutes. Many

Helostoma temmincki

pictures have been taken of this phenomena and have never failed to cause delighted comment.

Recently, these fish have been bred in quantities and are usually available. Lucky is the fancier who has a chance to add these hardy fish to this collection. Average size is 4 inches; some specimens and breeders up to 12 inches. Doesn't care for worms or live food.

BETTAS

FIGHTING FISH

The Prince of the Aquarium — The Veiltail Betta, which was selected as the frontispiece of this book, was first introduced into this country in 1927 from Siam by no less a personage than FRANK BUCK of "Bring 'Em Back Alive" fame. He turned them over to the importer, Mr. Locke of San Francisco, who subsequently bred them.

The original fish, *Betta splendens*, which has been known for years, was considered beautiful then because of the extraordinary coloring. Then, too, it has an added charm. Here was a fighter who only needed an opponent to give its all in a life-or-death

Betta splendens

battle. The natives of Siam bred the fish especially for this purpose and many large sums were wagered on the outcome. The fins were rather short. The body was formidable and the gill plates were movable and protruded in battle. Colors were solid and had quite a range — red, blue, green and cambodia. The last named is light with red anal, dorsal, ventrals and tail. High prices were asked with plenty of takers, as the supply was limited. Only one male could be put in a community aquarium. When once established, it was found to be an ideal mixer. Painstaking and selective breeding of this fish through the years developed the LO-FULLER. This variation gives a remarkable demonstration of ultra-selective breeding.

This constant breeding seems to have subdued the pugnacious nature of the fish. I have seen 2 domestic Bettas in the same tank staying at opposite ends. However, this is not advised, for if contact was established between them, shredding and tearing of the fins would result and often more serious wounds. This fish seems quite different from the originals. Fins are longer, tail and dorsal

LOFULLER — VEILTAIL BETTA

graceful and flowing, ventrals very pronounced. The magnificent colors are an artist's dream. Deep Reds, Royal Blues, Cool Sea Green, Brown and the Cambodia (a cream color with red ventrals, dorsal, tail, and anal). Since this fish needs very little water, it is at home in a small jar as well as a large tank. For this reason, decorators have installed them in many ways in home furnishings. At the base of a table lamp. Large electric light bulbs have been prepared and water added, with a bit-o'-plant and sand. Your choice of any color Betta made a novel addition to the surroundings. Females come in all colors, have stubby fins, rounded plump bodies and a white spot prominently displayed at the base of the breast. Breeding is easy, as they are bubble nest builders. Have the water slightly acid, plenty of plants and light and a good female. As young mature, put them in separate mason jars to bring them up to size and prevent fighting. Average size, 2½ inches.

The Siamese make use of the pugnacity of the males for betting. A good fish has often huge sums put on him. This is a unique position for a fish to occupy in the life of a people.

CHARACINS

CHARACINS or Egg-layers (as we refer to them) comprise a family that ranges from the Neon Tetra, with its exquisite color and adaptability to aquarium life, to the rugged, ferocious Piranha (better known as the "man-eating fish"), whose fierce nature makes it fight amongst its own kind.

Most Characins have friendly natures and get along well with other fish. But, in breeding, they present a tricky problem for all but the experienced breeder. Some, such as Hatchet Fish, Ulreyi and Pencil Fish, along with other popular varieties, have to be imported constantly to supply the demand. Since this is a difficult time to import fish, quite a number are temporarily off the market. However, it is best to list them as from time to time a shipment gets through and a lucky fancier, recognizing the fish and realizing its history, knows he has made a valuable addition to his aquarium.

Specimens are found in So. America and Africa. This does not mean that they require very warm water, as most Characins live comfortably in from 70 to 75 degrees. Breeding temperature around 80. They like live food best, but will eat what is available.

Breeding habits differ in Characins. But fundamental requirements are well-planted aquariums, water slightly acid, and male and female fish in good condition. This group presents many interesting features in breeding that more than repays the aquarist for his time and effort.

HYPHESSOBRYCON INNESI—MYERS

NEON TETRA

THIS fish is one of the most talked-about to date. Under collecting you learned about its discovery and hardships involved in importing.

The Neon is found in small tributaries of the Amazon, far into inaccessible country. This article gives the exact facts attendant on its arrival in this country and how the scientific and common names were obtained.

Mr. Rabaut, the collector and first man to discover the fish, on arriving in Paris with his second shipment, turned them all over to a dealer named LePant. This dealer, wishing to keep them off the market until they could be classified, asked a banker friend of his, J. S. Neel (who was quite a fancier), to keep the fish while inquiries were made. Mr. Neel not only jumped at the chance to care for these beauties, but wrote to William T. Innes (known as the father of the tropical fish hobby in this country) and offered to send several pair to him for classification. Mr. Innes, on receiving the fish, realized that here indeed was a new "star of the aquarium." His friend, Dr. Myers, classified them as the genus *Hyphessobrycon*. Since the species was not known, he added *innesi* after Mr. Innes. In all scientific names you will find the name of the ichthyologist who first classified the fish after the original. Thus the full title, *Hyphessobrycon innesi* -- Myers. The common name was the spontaneous response of Rabaut and LePant, who upon observing the Neon in all its glory were struck by the similarity to the Neon Light. At once they saddled it with the name "Neon Fish" and in most people's opinion this is indeed most appropriate.

To date, almost eight years after the Neon was first discovered, it is my sad duty to relate that this fish has very rarely been bred in quantity. Scattered reports have come in from breeders all over the country saying that they have bred the Neon, but the spawn was never large and the young developed very slowly. In my opinion, the imports are more beautiful and, despite their long voyage, very hardy.

When our illustrator brought in the color picture of the Neon for this book, I realized that he did not do full justice to the beauty

Hyphessobrycon innesi

Hyphessobrycon gracilis

Tanichthys albonubes

of the fish. It was drawn from life and unfortunately it is not possible to capture the elusive coloring of this beauty.

Sex determination is quite difficult in these fish and is done by observing their shape. The female is broad and much rounder than the male and, when ripe, belly is distended. Neons thrive on prepared food as well as Daphnia and as a special treat may be fed small worms from time to time. The average size is one inch. When full grown, 2 inches of beauty strike your eye.

The best method observed in breeding Neons is to use a 5-gallon aquarium. Omit gravel and put in Myriophyllum and Nitella. Select a pair not over one year old. If the male fails to drive the female after a lapse of 2 hours, remove the male and replace him with another. After spawning, both parents should be removed from the tank.

Before you decide to breed the Neons, however, be sure they are in good condition and well fed. The water should be 24 hours old and the temperature for breeding about 78 degrees. Twenty-four hours after the eggs are hatched start feeding newly hatched Brine Shrimps. Do not feed while the fish are in the breeding tank.

HYPHESSOBRYCON FLAMMEUS

RED OR TETRA VON RIO

THIS beauty from Rio de Janeiro has a dark red body and fins with 3 black bars on each shoulder. Presents a striking picture in the aquarium and its dainty movements and peaceful nature make it very popular. Likes Daphnia and all dried foods. Average size, one inch. Easy to breed; temperature, 70 to 75 degrees. Female is larger than the male and not so colorful. Body is broad and does not have the black edging on dorsal and anal fins that is found on the male. Use a 5-gallon tank, planted with quite a few bushy plants. Make sure fish are healthy and full bodied. These fish, as others of this group, spawn in the plant thickets. When this is completed, remove parents to avoid possible destruction to eggs or babies. The eggs hatch in about 72 hours and average about 400. The young are helpless at birth and stick to plants and sides of the aquarium. They absorb contents of the egg sac which takes several days. After this, they must be fed infusoria or very fine dried food. The young develop rapidly and show color after a few weeks. They are hardy and present a colorful picture in the aquarium. All Tetras enjoy plenty of light, a point to always keep in mind. Because of the easy way they breed, the TETRA VON RIO is always available.

HYPHESSOBRYCON GRACILIS
GLO-LITE TETRA

GRACILIS, meaning "graceful," starts us off on the description of this beautiful fish. The delicate blend of colors through the almost transparent body and the red-tinted fins show up especially well in properly lighted aquariums. The name GLO-LITE gives a better idea as to the glowing colors as seen in the illustration. This fish was an accidental discovery by a collector in Guiana and proved so popular zealous breeders, finding the fish was not too difficult to breed, produced them quite regularly, making it unnecessary to import them.

They breed like most Tetras, about 75 to 80 degrees. Are hardy and peaceful and eat most foods offered.

HEMIGRAMMUS ULREYI
HYPHESSOBRYCON HETERORHABDUS

SINCE these 2 fish are so similar, it is hard for anyone but an expert to tell them apart. We are mentioning them together to explain distinguishing features.

The *heterorhabdus*, while the same size and shape as the *ulreyi*, is not as vivid in coloring and has a black spot on the tail. Since it is a fish rarely seen and not as popular as the *ulreyi*, we will not mention it further.

The *ulreyi* has the beauty of the true aquarium fish from the Amazon and while rarely bred does not last long on the market when offered. A dark green body with gold stripe from gill to tail and red eyes make a pleasing blend. The male has a hook on the anal fin and more color than the female. Then, too, she is slightly larger. Peaceful natured fish with a wholesome appetite makes it unfortunate that they cannot be bred here. Temperature, 72 to 78 degrees. Length, 1½ inches.

HYPHESSOBRYCON PULCHRIPINNIS

LEMON TETRA

THE Lemon Tetra, while not as flashy as some of the other Tetras, nevertheless has the same hardy, active and peaceful nature. For the aquarist who likes the small Characins, it makes a pleasant contrast to their brilliant coloring. The lemon color predominates and varies to deep yellow in the anal fin. The eye is red with yellow half circle above. Tail and other fins are pale lemon color.

These fish have not been offered lately, but are seen from time to time. Can be bred, but they eat their eggs so fast it discourages breeders. Length, 1½ inches. Best temperature, 75 degrees. Eats well.

HYPHESSOBRYCON ROSACEUS

ROSY TETRA

THE *Rosaceus*, despite numerous attempts, has never been bred in quantities large enough to insure large distribution. It only appears now when an importer receives a shipment that includes them or a breeder with several batches at once. In any case, the *Rosaceus* never lasts long, as they are very desirable to the fancier

Hyphessobrycon rosaceus

because of their rare beauty. Their body is rose colored (hence *Rosaceus*), with bright red and orange fins. The erect dorsal has a blob of black color on it tipped with white (in females the dorsal is shorter, tipped with red). The tail has a light color with red and black edging. This is a remarkable blend of color. These fish are peaceful and eat anything. Temperature, 72 to 75 degrees. Another wonder fish of the far-reaching Amazon. Length, 2 inches.

HYPHESSOBRYCON PULCHER

RASBORA TETRA

THIS fish is of such recent origin, only one book to date lists it, and then very sketchily. First introduced about 1937, it was off the market and made several reappearances in the ensuing years. The name *pulcher* means "pretty," but we lean more to handsome. The body is a golden lemon color with red-tinted dorsal. Fins and tail are lemon colored. A blue-black wedge starts at tail and goes a short way into the body, ending abruptly. This is a distinctive marking that adds much to the general attractiveness of the fish. They attain 2 inches but average size is one inch. They have been bred here and in Europe and have a friendly nature and eat well. The black mark on the lower part of the body reminds one of the *Rasbora heteromorpha* (described under Barbs), therefore called Rasbora Tetra.

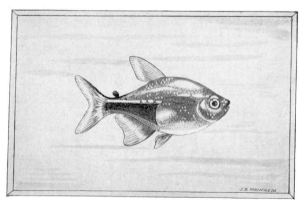

Hyphessobrycon pulcher

HYPHESSOBRYCON SERPAE

SERPAE MINOR

In general build and color this fish resembles the *rosaceus*, except for a salmon-colored sheen and a black spot on shoulder. Fins are reddish, dorsal not as large but same black spot. The *serpae* is rather timid and should be kept with fish his own size, about one inch. Easy to keep but hard to breed. When this is accomplished, young mature and are cared for in typical Tetra fashion. Likes daphnia and all dried foods and when once established in the aquarium, does very well.

HEMIGRAMMUS OCELLIFER

HEAD-AND-TAIL LIGHT

Here is an ideal community fish, hardy and active. Always available and peaceful. This is one of the most popular of the Characins and should be included in any collection of community fish. The body has a golden sheen and eyes are red with gold above. A short black line runs to base of tail, where a copper spot reflects the light, hence Head-and-Tail Light. As they swim about through the plants, the lights flash in unique fashion. Breed easily, as Tetras. Young mature fast. Temperature, 70 to 80 degrees. Length, 1½ inches. Female rounded body, paler in color.

PRISTELLA RIDDLEI

The *Pristella* is an old friend to most fanciers. Like the *ocellifer*, it goes to make up the average selection of fish for community aquariums. Friendly, active and easy to breed. Eats anything and has a temperature range of 10 degrees. Happiest at 75 degrees.

While the *Pristella* does not have vivid color, it has attractive markings, black spots on dorsal, anal and ventral fins with white-and-yellow spots above and below. Lower front of fish silver. Other part of body is a transparent brown, red tail, brownish dot behind eye that starts a faint line to the base of the tail. It provides a contrast when placed with brilliantly colored fish.

Hyphessobrycon bifasciatus
Hyphessobrycon pulchripinnis
Prionabrama filigera
Hyphessobrycon serpae
Hemigrammus unilineatus

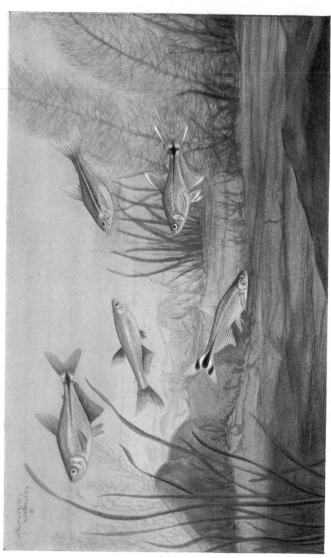

Hemigrammus caudovittatus   Hemigrammus ulreyi

Aphyocharax rubripinnis   Hemigrammus ocellifer

Hemigrammus rhodostomus

HEMIGRAMMUS RHODOSTOMUS
RUMMY-NOSE TETRA

A HUMORIST must have named this fish, for it does, indeed, have a red nose. Body color green with black-and-white markings on the tail. Fins reddish and upper part of body. This fish differs from the usual Tetra because of its long body and bulky appearance. Is quite delicate and, while bred, never very successfully. Any specimens offered are direct imports. Length up to 2 inches. Eats dried food, fleas and worms. Temperature about 75 degrees.

HEMIGRAMMUS CAUDOVITTATUS
TETRA FROM BUENOS AIRES

A VERY sociable fish, held rather cheaply by breeders because of prolific nature. Easy to breed, hardy and eats anything. Temperature, 65 to 75 degrees. Since this fish is the largest of the *Hemigrammus*, there are times when it has been caught nipping smaller fish. If kept with larger fish this will not happen. Length up to 3½ inches. Female slightly larger and fuller in outline. Color silver dorsal and anal reddish and colorful, distinctive mark at base of tail, blue-black diamond-shaped wedge that sends half line to middle of fish. Tail tinged with brilliant red. Always available.

GYMNOCORYMBUS TERNETZI
BLACK TETRA OR BLACKAMOOR

THE Black Tetra is a must for community tanks. No flashy pattern of colors, but a deep black from tip of the dorsal through the middle of the fish extending down to the lower fin and back to base of tail. Front half of body silver with two black bands on both sides. Tail so light as to be transparent. These fish, in a tank with the Red Tetra, provide a contrast that is striking when viewed with a background of plants and overhead light. The Black Tetras have been bred with great success and are considered ideal for home breeding. Breeders are from 1½ to 2 inches. The females are paler and at mating time exhibit a large abdomen. While dainty and peaceful by nature, they protect themselves quite well from more aggressive fish. Temperature, 75 to 80 degrees.

Gymnocorymbus ternetzi

APHYOCHARAX RUBROPINNIS
BLOODFINS

THE Bloodfins have different shaped bodies than the usual Tetras, but the adipose dorsal and anal fin of the Characin is present, leaving no doubt as to its identity. The body is silvery with blue-violet and red sheen. All fins are blood red, giving it the name and providing a contrast to the silver of the body. Breeding habits, like most Tetras. However, we recommend several pair be used in breeding, or 2 males to one female to fertilize the spawn. New water, 24 hours old, is especially suggested, as this serves to agitate the fish to greater efforts. They jump clear out of the water, their bodies coming in contact in the air. Eggs are tossed in all directions. Breeding Bloodfins is not only an accomplishment, but the fish themselves are ideal for aquarium life. Length, 1¾ inches.

GASTEROPELECUS LEVIS
WHITE HATCHET FISH

THIS strange member of the Characin group is the most common of the Hatchet Fish clan. The name Hatchet is derived from the thin body shape that suggests that implement. The graceful arching pectoral fins provide "wings" and the Hatchets have often been called "the fresh water flying fish." This is not true, however, as they do not "fly," but skim along the surface looking for food and insects. In aquarium life, they are most always to be found near the top and do not eat food once it gets on the bottom. They are very peaceful and add a novel note to the community aquarium.

Breeding is very difficult and very few aquarists have accomplished this feat. They must be imported and are short-lived fish. The author has seen numerous cases where these fish have lived in community aquariums for long intervals and almost doubled in size. The body is a metallic silver color with dark green top. A faint dark line separates these colors and extends to the base of the tail. Fins are almost transparent. These fishes attain a length of 3 inches. Like clear water, about 75 degrees. Eat most foods, particularly daphnia.

CARNEGIELLA STRIGATA

MARBLED HATCHET FISH

A PIECE of marble cake supplied the common name for this strangely colored Hatchet Fish. Black lines run through the fish in quite the same manner, against the silver background. A metallic line runs through the body from the base of the tail to the eye and, above this, dark green along the top. This fish, while smaller than the *levis*, is considered better to keep, as it is more lasting. Has been bred at about 85 degrees, but in very small quantities. Appears now and then, when shipments are received. The name *Carnegiella* is for Miss Margaret Carnegie. *Strigata* means streaked.

CARNEGIELLA MARTHAE

GLASS HATCHET FISH

THIS fish, named by Dr. G. S. Myers for his wife Martha, is the smallest and hardiest of the Hatchet Fish. It is very popular among fanciers. Survives cold and poor aquarium conditions. Likes dried

Carnegiella strigata
Pterodiscus levis
Carnegiella marthae
Chalcinus elongatus
Thoracocharax securis
Pseudocorynopoma doriae Female and Male
Corynopoma rissii Male and Female

food and daphnia. It averages 2 inches in size. The body is glass-like, almost opaque. The fins and wings are almost black. There is a black line along top of the fish and the sides are peppered with black flecks. Likes water about 75 degrees, but can withstand fluctuations of 10 degrees either way. The Hatchet Fish add distinctiveness to any aquarium.

NANNAETHIOPS UNITAENIATUS

AFRICAN TETRA

THIS colorful Characin is from far-off Africa, inhabiting the mucky waters of the Nile and Congo Rivers. Its body is long with a plump appearance and fins are well spread and erect as if it is constantly standing at attention. Hardy, peaceful and easy to breed make it a desirable fish for the fancier. Eats anything. Temperature about 75 degrees. Body color, pale gold. A black stripe goes through the middle from eye to tail. This stripe has a gold line about it that fades into red near the tail. Dorsal reddish with black edging. Breeds as Tetras, water about 80 degrees. Use a larger tank with bushy plants. Remove parents when spawning is over to prevent destruction and follow the directions for raising as in the other Characins.

HEMIGRAMMUS UNILINEATUS

FEATHER FINS

THIS fish, like the *ocellifer*, is both hardy and popular with aquarists. Easy to breed and always available. It is often confused with *Pristella riddlei*. The body is dark green with a silvery sheen. A line goes through the body of the fish and appears silver with black edging. Dorsal and anal fins have black markings. The tail is light red. A pretty fish that spawns easily (as *flammeus*) and young, being larger, mature quickly. Eats anything. Is peaceful and very active in the aquarium. Size from 1½ to 1¾ inches. Temperature from 70 to 80 degrees.

COPEINA GUTTATA

THE *Copeina*, as with the *Pristella*, has no common name. There are other varieties of *Copeina*, but this is the most popular, colorful and most often seen. We, therefore, chose it to represent the genus. The body is brown on top with a strong blue sheen below. The male has violet and red spots all over; however, very faintly on the female. The fins are yellow tipped with red. The male's color is highly intensified as breeding time nears. The eggs are laid in a hollow in the sand and the male guards them. A small plate, put on the bottom, will serve as a good receptacle for the eggs. This fish is not a fast swimmer, but is content to make his way very slowly around the aquarium. Can withstand cold or warm water anywhere in the sixties up to 90 degrees. Will eat anything and has a peaceful nature. Average size, 2½ inches. A good fish for the beginner to try to breed to observe interesting habits of the fish.

POECILOBRYCON AURATUS
PENCIL FISH

THE PENCIL FISH is unique in many ways. His long thin body is almost completely round and, instead of swimming in the conventional way, he goes through the water at almost a 45-degree angle. This presents a strange picture in the community aquarium. Fanciers are constantly on the lookout for this fish. However, due to breeding difficulties, specimens must be imported. They appear occasionally now, but when shipping problems are solved they will usually be available. Length, 1½ inches. Likes live food. Temperature 75 to 80 degrees. Slender Pencil shaped body, golden with brown stripes. A broad black stripe starts at the eye and goes down the length of the fish, blending into the lower half of the tail. The upper half is light gold. The dorsal and anal fins are tinged dark brown. Slow swimmers, rather timid. Larger fish take advantage of this trait.

POECILOBRYCON UNIFASCIATUS
PENCIL FISH

THIS and the *Auratus* are similar in size and shape. The difference being color and a more streamlined appearance. These attain 2

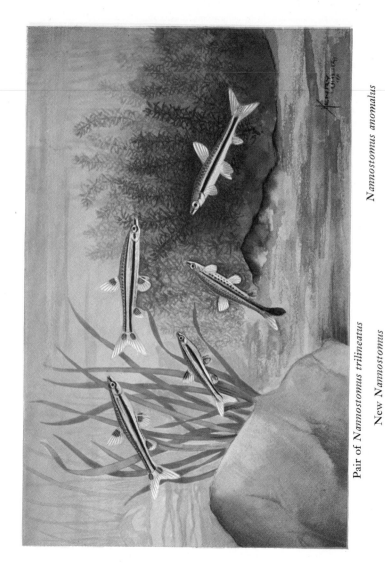

Pair of *Nannostomus trilineatus*   *Nannostomus anomalus*

New *Nannostomus*   *Poecilobrycon auratus*

inches. Their nature, eating habits and the temperature is the same as for the *auratus*. The broad black line extends from the tip of the nose through the eye and down to the end of the tail. The upper half of the body is brown, underside silver to white. The PENCIL FISH adds a touch of the unusual to an aquarium.

NANNOSTOMUS TRILINEATUS

THIS fish was first introduced over 10 years ago. But, to this day, has never been bred in quantities necessary to supply the general fancier who goes out of his way to obtain rare fish. It has been off the market for some time now, but we hope it will make its reappearance soon. The flashy colors of this fish are vivid and all the fins are splotched with deep red. The body is long and very graceful. From the tip of its small mouth to its beautiful tail the colors run riot. Three dark lines go through body from the red-tipped nose to tail. Above top line greenish brown, in between gold and below pale red. Eats anything, likes algae and is peaceful and quite hardy. Temperature, 70 to 80 degrees. Named *Nannostomus* for small mouth — *Trilineatus* means "three lined." Length, 1¾ inches.

NANNOSTOMUS MARGINATUS

THIS is the smallest of the *Nannostomus*, average size being one inch. The body is broader with 3 black stripes from the nose to the tail. Between these stripes, gold color. Below, silver stripes edged with red. The dorsal and ventral fins are bright red. General care as for *trilineatus*. An attractive community fish.

HEMIODUS SEMITAENIATUS

THIS fish wears that tired look. Its long body seems to curve, giving it a dejected appearance. This is belied, however, when an attempt is made to catch it. Then it springs to life and in trying to elude the net may jump out of the aquarium or container in which it had been placed. It fits well with community fish and its long silvery body, with black dot and short black line to lower lobe of the tail, provides a contrast to brilliantly colored fish. Likes daphnia but will eat all dried foods. Never bred successfully. Therefore, not often seen on the market. Grows to 5 inches. Temperature, 75 degrees.

HEMIODUS OBLIQUITHAYARI

THIS is a more recent *Hemiodus* that surpasses the *semitaeniatus* for beauty and grace. It has the same long body, but filled out more, with a deep black stripe that starts under the gill and traverses lower part of the body, continuing through the lower lobe of the tail. The upper part of the tail is almost transparent. The back is a dark, bronzed green, while the lower part of the body is yellowish to olive green. Lives long and well. Eats whatever offered. Swims with the head at a slightly upward angle. Breeds easily if a well-matched pair can be obtained.

ANNOSTOMUS ANNOSTOMUS

THE fish, with the double name, obtained same because of his turned-up mouth, meaning *Annostomus*. This is more of a show fish for large aquariums containing big fish. When put with smaller fishes it is liable to nip their fins. The peculiar feature of this fish is that it swims with its head down and body slightly arched. Eats well, all types of food, particularly worms. No information is available on breeding. I don't think that it has been accomplished to any great degree, if at all. Very colorful and sought after for rare show fish. May be seen in large Public Aquariums throughout the country. Length, 4 inches. Best temperature, 75 degrees.

LEPORINUS FASCIATUS

THIS is a fish that is rarely seen of late, never having been bred to this writer's knowledge. Collectors relate it is quite difficult to obtain and transport. The stories of the leaping prowess of the fish are told and retold and brings to mind an experience I had some years ago in the large wholesale Aquarium where I worked.

Leporinus fasciatus
Leporinus affinis
Leporinus friderici
Leporinus leschenaultii

Our tanks were in tiers, 3 high, and we had row after row. I placed a *Leporinus* in a top tank and the following morning found the fish several rows away. Thinking someone had moved it, I placed it back in the same tank. Several hours later I heard a loud "plop." Upon investigation, there was the *Leporinus* in a bottom tank that contained a pretty shaky lot of Gold Guppies. This fish has tremendous power to lift himself out of the water and clear the top of the tanks — we only kept the tanks one-half to three-fourths full. Moral — always have the aquarium covered, as several types of community fish are good jumpers!

The *Leporinus* has a golden color with black bands around the body from the nose to the tail. As the fish matures more bands appear up to 10. Swims head-down fashion as the *Annostomus*. Eats anything but prefers worms. It is a good species for an aquarium containing large fish. Peaceful and very hardy. Length to 6 inches.

PROCHILODUS INSIGNIS
FLAG FISH

THIS fish has a flag-striped tail that gave it the common name. There was another fish with this same appellation which has long since vanished from the community aquarium. We therefore allow the *Prochilodus* use of this distinguished title. The name *insignis* means "distinguished," so it is only fitting to combine the two. The tail is the outstanding feature, as the body colors are not bright, but sort of pale red with a metallic sheen. Dorsal and lower fins are a pale yellow. The lower lip projects forward. In aquariums it attains a length of about 5 inches. In natural surroundings, 11 inches. Recommended for large aquariums. It is peaceful with fish of its own size, likes worms and algae. Will also eat dried food. This fish will jump if the aquarium is left uncovered.

CHILODUS PUNCTATUS
HEAD STANDER

WHILE the *Prochilodus* and the *punctatus* are not to be had at the time of this writing, we see them often enough to know there is

Chilodus punctatus
Hemiodus semitaeniatus
Prochilodus insignis
Prochilodus taeniurus

a definite demand for both. Both must be imported, as breeders have tried time and again to get large spawns for the commercial market without success. This fish swims in a head-down position and goes his way in that fashion feeling very natural. A contrast from one extreme to another is this fish in an aquarium with the "head-up — tail-down" PENCIL FISH. The *punctatus* has a glossy sheen in which several colors merge. A black stripe starts at the mouth and runs through the middle in a straight line to the tail. The upper half of the body is reddish brown. The dorsal is spotted with black at the tip. Other fins are pale red. A novel and colorful fish, peaceful and hardy. Average size, 2½ inches. Likes algae, worms and live food. At best in water temperature from 75 to 80 degrees.

SERRASALMUS PIRAYA
PIRANHA

THE MAN-EATER OF THE AMAZON — What visions do words such as these conjure in the mind's eye? Surely a large, terrible-looking fish, with row upon row of sharp, vicious teeth, capable of biting a man in two!

On the contrary, the Piranha averages only 10 inches in size, belongs to the friendly Characin Family and its appearance certainly belies such a forbidding name. However, tributaries of the upper Amazon, that contain these fish, are shunned by natives and animals alike. Woe betide the luckless creature that falls into these streams. Thousands of hungry Piranhas congregate at that spot and in a matter of minutes, with tiny bites, they reduce the body to a skeleton.

Their insatiable appetites cause them to fight with one another, and the losers become meals for the stronger ones in a constant "survival of the fittest."

Very prolific in natural haunts, the Piranha has never been bred in captivity. When these fish are collected, size cannot vary more than 2 inches, as the larger Piranha would kill the smaller ones en route. All these fish bear scars of battle and have remarkable recuperative powers. They rarely die a natural death, for obvious reasons.

Stories and pictures of these fish have been widely circulated and most large Public Aquariums have several on display. They are an invaluable attraction with a dramatic history.

METYNNIS ROOSEVELTI

THIS *Metynnis* was named for a rugged fighter, Theodore Roosevelt, and has some of the same qualities in a smaller degree. While not good community fish, some fanciers keep only several varieties of *Metynnis* in their tank, as they are larger and have a rare quality that intrigues some people possessing special collections. They are noted as ravenous plant eaters and are displayed in tanks with this in mind. This fish has rarely been bred in captivity, a fact which keeps advanced fanciers trying to be the first to find the ideal aquarium conditions that will result in large spawns regularly. Length up to 6 inches. Very hardy; temperature, 70 to 80 degrees. The silver, disc-shaped body of this fish is dotted with round black spots of varied size. The large anal fin is orange with red edging. The tail is orange, outer edge black. The peculiar dorsal is edged with black. Besides plants for food, the *roosevelti* likes all types of live food and prepared dried foods.

METYNNIS MACULATUS

THE *maculatus* looks like the *roosevelti*, but is smaller and the spots are more pronounced with a half moon black spot behind the gill cover. The specimens offered are about 2 inches and have been introduced in community aquariums with fish of this size and lived peacefully. However, as size increases, their appetite for plants seems to increase. When this is first observed, try feeding lettuce or other greens. This may change their eating habits and save decorative plants. General care as for the *roosevelti*. Very hardy.

METYNNIS SCHREITMUELLERI

THIS *Metynnis* is the large member of the genus. Has been seen up to 12 inches in length. In my talks with collectors I was quite surprised to learn that this was a food fish and natives in certain parts of So. America eat them quite regularly. Many beautiful specimens have been displayed in large aquariums throughout the country. However, they have not been on the market for some time. Since all *Metynnis* come from the Amazon basin, future

Metynnis roosevelti
Metynnis maculatus
Metynnis schreitmuelleri
Serrasalmus piraya

imports from there will probably include some of these interesting fish. This variety has a deep, silvery body, almost flat, with greenish metallic gleam, hooked anal fin which is bright red. Dorsal is spotted and edged with black. The tail has a black fringe. Plants are the main diet of this fish and the author has seen planted aquariums torn and ravaged after this fish was introduced by mistake. Hardy and active.

CICHLIDS

THIS family provides interesting specimens for the fancier and has outstanding characteristics and breeding habits. A great majority are peaceable and fit well in community aquariums, while others are more pugnacious, but are kept for their beauty with members of their own species.

Cichlids are usually found in So. America, but some specimens come from Africa, India and our own Texas, being found in the Rio Grande River. The males, during courtship, display such fervor that the poor female presents a rather battered appearance after mating is complete. Most Cichlids have similar breeding habits. Therefore, this description will fit nearly all of them with the exception of the Mouthbreeders, which will be discussed together with the description of these unique fish. Since most Cichlids are hard to sex, it is well to buy a mated pair or purchase several and watch for them to mate or flirt with each other. This signifies the fish are ready to breed.

The male develops brilliant color and dashes against the female in an effort to get her to reciprocate. When she is ready, she returns the affection. Have a 10-gallon tank handy, or larger, if possible, filled with water not over 48 hours old (a popular misconception is that old water is needed for Cichlids), and between 78 and 82 degrees in temperature, about 3 inches of sand on the bottom (Cichlids like to dig holes in the sand) and no plants. Provide a good light for the aquarium and introduce breeders. These fish clean the place where the eggs are to be deposited with scrupulous care. It must be spotless. When all this is done to complete satisfaction, the female begins depositing eggs. The male follows immediately and sprays them with its fertilizing fluid. This is repeated until the female stops. Then both fish fan the eggs with fins and tail as though breathing life itself into them.

Eggs usually hatch in 3 or 4 days and again the parents take charge. They move them from hole to hole in the sand with methodical precision, carrying them in their mouth (authorities on these fish state that this process acts as a bath for the fish). When the yolk sacs have been absorbed by the young fish, they swim right up around their parents and get in formation. Swimming around in this fashion, it is delightful to watch the stragglers shot back in place from the mouth of either parent. Both male and female are highly conscious of their duty as parents and it warms one's heart to see this highly developed trait so prevalent in fish in our own aquariums. Parents resent any intrusion from anyone during this period. Therefore, guide your actions accordingly if you are ever fortunate enough to have these fish breed for you. It will be a delightful and fascinating experiment you will never forget. When young are free of yolk sac, feed infusoria or fine daphnia.

Parents may be removed any time after this. However, care must be exercised not to scare them, as they may eat the babies to save them from harm.

PTEROPHYLLUM SCALARE

ANGEL FISH

THIS Cichlid is one of the most popular aquarium fishes, being seen in practically every tank with a community collection.

The majestic bearing and graceful motions of the fish have resulted in it being called "the king of the aquarium," and its haughty demeanor seems to bear this out, as though it were conscious of this royal title.

There are 3 varieties of this fish available from time to time, but most common and easiest to breed is the *eimekei*, which we shall describe here. The true P. *scalare* is seldom bred and the P. *altum* is also very difficult. Both fish resemble the *eimekei* except for minor differences in body shape and fins. For years all Scalares had to be imported direct as they were thought impossible to breed. But experimentation continued and now thousands and thousands are being bred yearly. I was fortunate in being able to visit a large hatchery in Ardsley, N. Y., recently, and the scientific method employed in breeding Scalares was a revelation. Each tank in this

Pterophyllum scalare

Pterophyllum altum

Pterophyllum eimekei

certain section contained Scalares in various stages of growth. On each tank was a tag, giving the date of birth and data as to the parents. On the breeders' tank, the tag attached told when they had been bred last. Each pair rests for a certain period before being allowed to spawn again. All babies had good fins and healthy bodies from the 20-day size up. Their lives are regulated scientifically until old enough to be offered on the market. Breeding methods such as these have brought the price of Scalares down quite a bit, so that many more people can now enjoy the fish that were heretofore considered expensive. I know the men who make this possible, feel that their efforts in this direction are worth while.

The Scalare has a small, flat body, with very long fins and a well-developed tail. A pear-shaped appearance makes it appear much larger than it actually is. Size averages from 2 to 3 inches. Its silver body has several black bands that extend into fins. The base of the tail has a black spot. Its feelers, when fully developed, measure 4 or 5 inches.

In breeding the Scalare, it is advisable to have acid water, about 6.6 pH. A testing kit is necessary here. Put plants such as broad-leaf Sagittaria or Vallisneria in the tank, as these fish lay their eggs on the plant leaves. Breeding from here on the same as previously described. Scalares are hardy, good eaters, prefer live food and a temperature of about 75 degrees. Large specimens must be kept with fish of their own size, as they often nip smaller fish, particularly the Betta, who fights back and either one gets hurt in the exchange.

SYMPHYSODON DISCUS

BLUE SCALARE OR POMPADOUR FISH

This is truly a rare fish. It is the dream of the fancier, who maintains a large aquarium with selected specimens of spectacular beauty, to possess a pair of these aristocrats. When first introduced about 10 years ago prices were quoted in 3 figures and all those available were sold. Succeeding importations brought the price down somewhat, but it is still in the expensive fish class.

Although this fish breeds like the Scalare, it has rarely been bred successfully. The parents eat the eggs or the young die off early. Recent shipments have not included the *discus*, probably because

Symphysodon discus

of their size (5 to 6 inches), as the valuable space is being needed for larger quantities of Neons, Pencils, etc., which can be packed in smaller spaces with no ill effects. The *discus* resembles a colored pancake, being flat. The body color varies, burnt orange with blue-black stripes, head and back with shining blue bands. The ventral and anal fins are wine red and blue. The female's body color is dull yellow. Likes live food and is a hardy, gentle fish that wouldn't harm a Guppy. Best temperature, 75 to 85 degrees. One of the most beautiful fish to come out of the Amazon. We hope to see it again soon.

CICHLASOMA FESTIVUM
MESONAUTA INSIGNIS

DISTINCT markings are a feature of this fish. A black stripe starts at the mouth and extends up to the point of the dorsal. The body is silver with olive overcast. Dark bands around the body that fade as they increase in size. Feelers extend from the ventrals but

Cichlasoma festivum

not as long as on the P. Scalare, long dorsal and anal, black spot at the base of the tail. Breeds as per description of Cichlids, but results are uncertain. Likes all live food and coarse dried food. Hardy and peaceful with fish of its own size. Best temperature, 72 to 80 degrees. Length, 4 inches.

CICHLASOMA CUTTERI

WHILE there are many fish of the genus Cichlasoma, we will not attempt to list them all. The several listed here are fairly popular and less pugnacious than the others, as is the case with the *cutteri*. These fish breed readily and fit well into the peaceful life of the

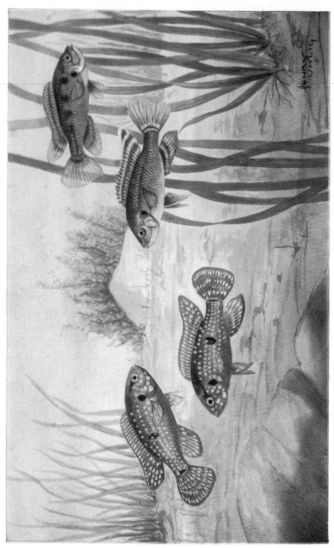

Pair of *Hemichromis bimaculatus*
Pair of *Haplochromis multicolor*

home aquarium. They are recognized immediately by the 7 dark bars through the body against a blue-green background. These are more prominent in the female as breeding time approaches and fade away to a faint shadow in the male. Both have a black spot at the base of the tail and an unusual blue circle around their green eyes. Breeding as described. Eggs hatch in 36 hours at temperature around 80 degrees. These fish have bred in a community tank with other fish, contrary to the usual nature of Cichlids. Hardy and long lived. Eat anything. Average size, 2½ inches.

HAPLOCHROMIS MULTICOLOR

MOUTHBREEDER

In previous descriptions of fish and breeding habits the advice, "Remove parents as they eat the eggs," is usually included. This will not be necessary here. This female, our Egyptian Mouthbreeder, performs a heroic duty in spawning and hatching her young.

To breed, condition the pair well, especially the female. Place the pair in a 5- or 10-gallon aquarium with a few plants. Have a sandy bottom, as the fish will make a depression in the sand to deposit the eggs. Be certain the female is full and well fed before breeding is attempted. The courtship is uneventful, male circles the female, fanning a depression in the sand, as she drops several eggs. Then begins the strange procedure that is to last for over 14 days and which establishes the female as one of the strangest, most sacrificing mothers in aquarium history. As the eggs are fertilized, she picks them up in her mouth, repeating this process until all are laid (usually 80 or 90). These remain in her mouth while they hatch and yolk sacs are absorbed. For this 2-week period the mother does not touch food in any form and her body wastes away. Only her head and large mouth seem to remain the same. She moves her mouth quite frequently during this time to provide circulation for the eggs, to keep them clean and possibly to exercise her tired jaws. When the young are ready to venture forth, she opens her mouth and out they come into the new world. A sudden scare and back in a flash to mother's mouth! They keep returning until they are too large to all fit in. Then mother's job is done. When the babies appear, feeding may be started with fine Daphnia, Infusoria or dried food and some white worms for the female. Since the male has very little to do, it is best to remove it after spawning is completed.

"Multicolor" aptly describes these fish, as the body is silver, dark on top with shades of blue, green and pink on the sides and head. The fins are erect and colorful, while the tail is light red and blue.

A delightful, interesting fish for the beginner. Hardy and peaceful. Eats anything. Temperature, 70 to 80 degrees.

ETROPLUS MACULATUS
ORANGE CHROMIDE

This is a colorful, peaceful Cichlid from far-off India that would be very popular if it were always available. May be kept in a community collection and has even asserted its prolific nature by breeding in a tank with other fish. Breeding and care as described under Cichlids, but likes a small pot or rockwork on which to deposit eggs. These eggs seem to be hanging from threads when observed. The female is very attentive to the young and the male guards the family from harm. A very interesting fish to breed and very brilliantly colored at mating time. When breeders are available again, fanciers will see that a domestic supply is always on hand.

The body color is burnt orange with a black spot on each side. Small black dots appear as the fish matures. Fins are orange with red edging and the eye is bright red. The female is somewhat pale, but has same coloring as the male. The caudal on the female is usually white. Average size, 3 inches. A hardy fish that eats anything, but prefers live food and worms. The stiff fin rays give it the name *Etroplus*. *Maculatus* means "with spots." Temperature, 70 to 80 degrees.

ASTRONOTUS OCELLATUS
PEACOCK-EYE CICHLID OR MARBLE CICHLID

The first time the author saw these fish they were part of a "just arrived" So. American shipment. The pair were beautiful speci-

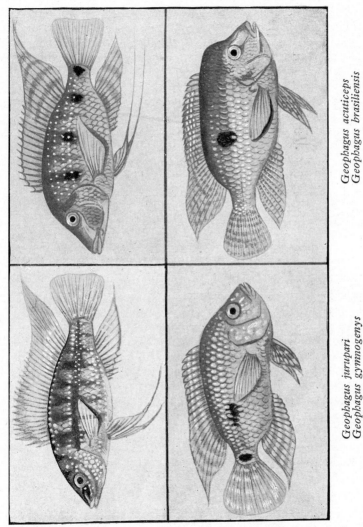

Geophagus acuticeps
Geophagus brasiliensis

Geophagus jurupari
Geophagus gymnogenys

mens, already sold to the Shedd Aquarium, Chicago. They were 10 inches long, velvety black with erect fins and a peacock eye set at the base of the tail. Several starlike white spots were seen on the body and behind the eye. The collector informed me these fish, in their natural surroundings, attain 16 inches. Several months later another shipment contained 300 fish about 2½ inches that looked vaguely familiar. Upon closer examination I found these were the baby *Astronotus*. Friendly, hardy little fish with silver and black markings like marble cake. They won instant approval from dealers and fanciers and were put in many community aquariums. However, as they grow larger, they sometimes nip the fins of other fish, a trait usually noted in all Cichlids to some degree.

The *Astronotus* have been successfully bred by experts and very large spawns were obtained. Hatching occurs about 3 days after eggs are laid. Parents must be watched as they eat the eggs if disturbed. Prefer live food such as worms and large daphnia. Specimens over 6 inches eat fish up to one inch in size as well as raw bits of meat. Temperature, 70 to 80 degrees.

GEOPHAGUS JURUPARI

THE *Geophagus jurupari* has not been seen recently but will appear in future shipments. This is another strange member of the family. Its head is pointed, unlike the usual blunt-faced Cichlids. The dorsal fin looks like a row of quills set in the back. Body is bright gold with scaly blue spots. Dark bands are around the body, fins are overcast with blue color. The mouth comes to a point with rather thick lips. Is considered peaceful and has been bred by interested breeders. Should be kept with large fish as the average size is 5 inches. A nicely colored fish with erect fins. Its popularity will grow with its repeated appearances. Very hardy, likes live food. Does not eat or disturb plants. From the Amazon. *Geophagus* meaning "earth eater," *jurupari* meaning "Devil's bait" (a native name). Temperature, 70 to 80 degrees.

CICHLASOMA MEEKI

FIREMOUTH CICHLID

THIS is the most colorful of the genus and very popular with

Aequidens curviceps
Etroplus maculatus

fanciers and breeders. In the flashy class. Large fish of this type have won prizes at many shows. The main feature of both fish is the fiery orange red breast that almost flames during mating. Next a dark spot with green edging is noted at the base of the gill plate. The dorsal, tail and anal fin is orange red tipped with blue. The ventrals are curved, red with a blue cast. The males have a long point at the rear of the dorsal fin which makes sex determination easy. Breeds as other Cichlids. Very prolific, hardy and a peaceful community fish. Best temperature, 75 to 80 degrees. Eats anything. Always available. Average size, 3 inches. Grows to 5 inches. The *meeki* is the only fresh-water fish with a red mouth.

AEQUIDENS CURVICEPS

ACARA THAYERI

This fish is also known as the Blue Acara, as the blue color is distributed through the body and all fins. Across the back greenish-brown blends into the light blue sides and the underparts are pink. Anal and ventral fins greenish color towards edge, tail light green with blue markings. A very pretty fish for the community aquarium. Breeding is a challenge to the fancier as the fish will eat the eggs after spawning. Best temperature, 75 degrees. Size about 2½ inches. Likes live food, dried food at intervals. Breeding as described.

AEQUIDENS PORTALAGRENSIS

The long second name of this fish explains its origin — Porto Alegre, Brazil. However, it breeds so easily and has such big spawns, we find it totally unnecessary to travel such a distance to obtain this colorful Cichlid. Like the previous *Aequidens*, this fish is also referred to as the Blue Acara because of their similarity. As most of the Acaras have blue in their varied colors, we will not make an attempt to put this common name on a certain fish.

Body color brassy-green, dark green stripe from eyes to base of the tail, underparts light blue. All fins and tail are green with blue running through. Since spawns are large, it is a pretty sight to see the parents guarding their offspring, usually over 100 babies. These mature rapidly. Average size of adult fish, 4 inches. Temperature, 75 to 80 degrees. Good eaters, peaceful and popular in community aquariums. Always available.

HEMICHROMIS BIMACULATUS

RED CHROMIDE OR JEWEL FISH

THE popularity of this fish is dimmed somewhat by its savage nature. A fighter so beautiful, beginners have tried to introduce them in community aquariums with disastrous results. The splendid blend of colors, with red predominating, and the interesting breeding habits are what saved the Jewel Fish from banishment. Many fanciers have separate tanks for keeping and breeding the Jewels, and a tank containing them alone provides the utmost in color and interest. Easy to breed, but selection of pairs must be left to nature. The male sometimes kills several females before it decides on its true love. Once mated, they should never be separated. This is true of most Cichlids.

Before breeding, condition both fish by feeding live food of all types, also some dried food. This insures the process and strengthens both fish for what lies ahead.

Breeding the Jewel Fish is one of the greatest pleasures possible for the fancier, and watching the tender demonstrations of the happy parents as they instruct their babies is indeed a touching sight. They breed as other Cichlids, but must not be disturbed. A sudden scare may result in the loss of an entire family, as the parents, if alarmed, may swallow every baby to save them from harm.

The body of the Jewel Fish, both male and female, is fiery red, covered with a pattern of pearly white and light blue spots. These extend to the dorsal, anal and ventral fins. The tail is orange red with faint black edging. A large black spot appears on both sides of the fish at intervals. The movements of these fish around the aquarium are like rare jewels flashing in the light. New colors are seen and disappear, to be replaced by brighter ones. A tank of Jewel Fish must really be seen in order to be appreciated. Average size, 2½ inches. Always available. Has quite a temperature range, making it very hardy, 65 to 85 degrees.

APISTOGRAMMA AGASSIZI

DWARF CICHLIDS

THE Dwarf Cichlids, of which there are several, appear on the market from time to time. The *agassizi* is the most popular, due to its beautiful colors and shy nature. Fins are long and flowing, tail is fan shaped with a point at the end. Body is yellow and reddish. Lower fins are orange, while the dorsal is orange tipped with red. A brilliant fish. Average size, 1½ inches. Can be bred in small tanks easily, as described under Cichlids. Place a small flower pot, tilted, in the aquarium as a place for the female to deposit her eggs. Very peaceful, hardy, eats anything. A smaller *Apistogramma* is the *pertense*. Very shy and not so colorful. Another is the mystery Cichlid, *Apistogramma U. 2. unknown.* Yellow, red and blue blend to show this fish at his best. All Dwarf Cichlids are hardy and are peaceful in community aquariums.

CYPRINIDAE

BARBUS VARIETIES

THIS family provides a wealth of color and interest for the community aquarium. Most specimens are hardy and prolific and are peaceful to a marked degree. While not considered "easy" to breed, once this is accomplished the fancier should have no further trouble. Others are practically impossible to breed and are only seen when imported. General breeding habits included here will be referred to when fish described are in this category. Sex is rather difficult to distinguish in these fish, but color and body contour is the deciding factor.

When a large female is observed, place it in a separate tank with one or 2 strong healthy males. Tank must be densely planted, as parents will eat the eggs immediately after spawning if they are easily found. The males chase the female till it becomes excited. It then sprays eggs in all directions among plants. These are adhesive and stick where they touch.

Remove parents when spawning is complete. Eggs left to themselves hatch in about 2 days and at that time can be fed infusoria. The young are hardy and mature quickly. This family needs very little attention and will eat all types of food. Breeding temperature between 75 and 80 degrees.

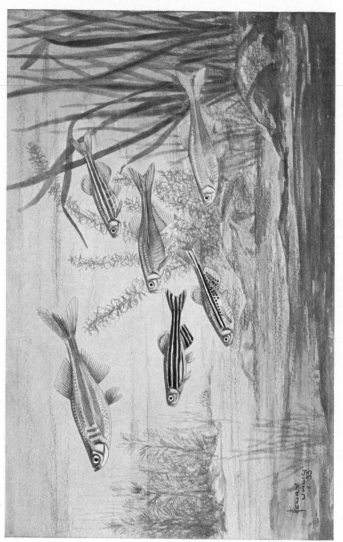

Danio malabaricus   Brachydanio rerio-albolineatus-Hybrid
Branchydanio rerio   Brachydanio albolineatus
Brachydanio nigrofasciatus   Gold Danio

DANIO MALABARICUS
GIANT DANIO

THIS colorful fish grows larger than most Danios. Hence its name Giant, usually seen at about 3 inches. A fast swimmer, its flashy colors and peaceful nature make it a "must" for community aquariums. As a rule it is found in the upper reaches of the tank. Breeding is fairly easy, as described under "Barbs." Always available because of this. The body is Salmon colored on top with several gold lines through the middle. The underside is silvery. All fins are slightly red, which at breeding time is highly intensified in the male. The female at this time becomes pale and full around belly. It is slightly larger than the male. All types of food may be fed. Best temperature, 70 to 80 degrees.

BRACHYDANIO RERIO
ZEBRA FISH

THESE tiny Danios average one inch in size and rare, indeed, is the community aquarium that does not boast of several of these energetic striped fish. Top swimmers. They flash back and forth and a school of 4 or 6 make quite a display. Body color is blue with silver stripes throughout. Very prolific, easy breeders as described. Hardy, peaceful and good eaters. They eat any food offered. Temperature, 70 to 80 degrees.

BRACHYDANIO ALBOLINEATUS
PEARL DANIO

IN size and shape the Pearl Danio is very much like the Zebra. Has the same peaceful nature and breeding habits. However, the delicate pearly lavender of the body is individual, and a reddish tint near the tail starts a line that extends through the tail, making a very attractive blend of color. Like other Danios, these fish originally came from India. But their prolific nature makes importations totally unnecessary. A variation of the Pearl Danio was produced by selective breeding. This fish is known as the GOLD DANIO. Body color is gold with light pink top and bottom. A very pretty fish. Keeping, breeding and habits as for Pearl Danio.

BRACHYDANIO ANALIPUNCTATUS
SPOTTED DANIO

SOMEWHAT like the Zebra and Pearl, the Spotted Danio presents a problem at breeding time. The best time to spawn the Spotted Danio is in the early Fall. If the female is right for breeding and is not being spawned it will become egg-bound. It is recommended to use 2 males to one female when breeding is attempted. However, it is suggested breeding the other Danios before this species in order to gain experience.

Lower portion of the body is white with black spots. Above this, blue and white stripes separate the light green upper half. Lively, hardy and peaceful. This is the smallest of the Danio clan. Breeders have crossed the Danios, but nothing startling has developed. Temperature, 70 to 80 degrees.

ORYZIAS LATIPES
GOLD MEDAKA

THIS pale gold Asiatic fish does not compare with most aquarium inhabitants for beauty, but its novel spawning habits keep up its popularity. When spawning, the males chase the females in Danio fashion, but the female at the height of its excitement, instead of spraying the eggs, expells them, where they stick to the long vent, much as a cluster of tiny pearls. These are brushed off within 10 or 12 hours on the aquarium plants, where they remain for about 8 days before hatching. The parents may be left in the tank as they will not eat their eggs. Beginners appreciate this fish as breeding is easy and fish are prolific. Valuable experience is gained that can be used on more difficult fish. The female can be distinguished by its short dorsal and round full body. The Medaka are very peaceful. Eat any type of food and have quite a temperature range, 50 to 80 degrees. Breeding temperature, 70 degrees.

TANICHTHYS ALBONUBES—LIN
WHITE CLOUD MOUNTAIN FISH

SOMEWHAT like the Neon Tetra, this fish has a fascinating history. Discovered in 1932 by a Chinese boy scout named Tan, in the

White Cloud Mountains near Canton, China, it was hailed by aquarists in this country upon its introduction here. Similar to the spotted Danio in size and shape, it was classified as a Brachydanio species. Lin Shu-Yen, head of the Fisheries Experiment Station, at Canton, named the fish *Tanichthys albonubes*. Lin, a name that is self-explanatory; *Tan*, discoverer; *ichthys*, Tan's fish; *Albonubes*, meaning White Cloud. The color illustration does not exaggerate the beauty of this fish. The natural delicate coloring was captured by the artist from a live subject and we present it as a true portrait of this brilliant Chinese addition to our community aquarium. Happily enough, the White Cloud proved itself to be hardy, peaceful and an easy, prolific breeder (Danio fashion), a fact that caused breeders no end of joy, as they are able to reproduce them often enough to supply the constant demand of the eager fanciers. To determine sex, mature fish must be used. The males have larger and more colorful fins, while the female is pale and very full around the body. Breeding is Danio fashion. Myriophyllum is suggested as the proper plant. A 5- or 10-gallon tank may be used, water slightly alkaline, about 80 degrees. Use 2 males to one female. Parents will not eat eggs if kept well fed on Daphnia or other live food. The babies show color right away and are much more brilliant than the parents, somewhat like young Neon Tetras. This color diminishes slightly as they grow older. Average size, 1½ inches. Eats anything and has a temperature range of 35 degrees, from 50 to 85.

BARBUS SUMATRANUS

RED FIN BARB

THE *Sumatranus* is one of the most popular "Barbs" used in community aquariums. Always available because of easy breeding habits. The average size offered are from three-quarters of an inch to one inch. These live happily and peacefully with other fish and eat all types of food. Most Barbus have a reputation of being pugnacious toward slower-moving fish, such as Bettas and Scalares. This, however, is only observed in large breeding specimens from 2½ to 3 inches and then only in individual fish. So we can safely

Barbus sumatranus

say that they are good community fish and are included in the average collection.

Females of this species must be conditioned before breeding, placed apart from other fish and fed plenty of live food. They are paler than the male and will show a fuller outline that grows larger as breeding time nears. A strong, healthy male is used. These, when placed in a 10-gallon, thickly planted aquarium, start a long courtship that continues until the female is exhausted and hovers over a thicket of plants. Quiveringly it expels the eggs, several at a time, among the plants. This continues for about 2 hours, until a few hundred eggs have been laid. When this process is complete, remove both parents, as they will look for and eat the eggs almost immediately. The young, tiny glass slivers, very hard to see, hatch in about 36 hours and cling to the sides of the aquarium. Feeding and care as described under Barbus varieties. Best breeding temperature is 80 degrees. Water slightly acid.

BARBUS OLIGOLEPIS

TIGER BARB

THIS pretty Barb, copper colored, with a silvery metallic sheen underneath, provides an interesting addition to community aquariums. The orange dorsal with a black border makes it stand out in mixed groups. The tail and fins vary from orange to deep red. Females can be easily distinguished. A silvery color predominates and several black spots are seen on her sides. The *oligolepis* average 1½ inches and are very hardy and peaceful. Will eat anything. They breed the same as *sumatranus*, but not as readily. The color in the male is highly intensified at breeding time. Bits of blue and green appear on the body. Temperature from 65 to 75 degrees. *Barbus* means "barbels on the nose"; *oligolepis* means large scales.

BARBUS EVERETTI

CLOWN BARB

THIS fish, because of its size and showy colors, is often used for exhibition purposes. Colors become more intense as size increases and at 5 inches the Clown Barb is really a beauty. Should be kept with fish of like size, in a 15-gallon aquarium or larger if possible. Very hardy and peaceful. If small specimens can be obtained, they fit well in the average collection. The large characteristic spots and general markings gave it the common name Clown Barb. This species has 2 pairs of barbels. Breeding as "Barbs," but a large, well-planted tank is necessary and pairs must be healthy and well fed. Breeding temperature, 80 degrees. Body color burnt orange, blue-black spots and markings over body. All fins blood red in mature fish. Very attractive against well-planted background. The top of the aquarium should be covered as they are jumpers.

BARBUS TICTO

THE outstanding feature of this "Barb" is the brilliant red of the dorsal fin in the male. At breeding time this color is highly pronounced. The female's dorsal is without color. Both fish have metallic bodies with 2 black spots and light pink fins. Hardy and peaceful and prolific, it is ideal for the novice. Eats anything. Breeding and keeping as "Barbs." Average size, 2 inches. Temperature, 72 to 80 degrees. Originally imported from Ceylon, India.

BARBUS NIGROFASCIATUS
STRAWBERRY BARB

THE *Nigrofasciatus*, in full color, is like a ripe strawberry. The males, at breeding time, show this color, and the erect dorsal, with its deep red with black edging and other fins so clear, make an unforgettable sight. Four dark bands are on the body, which remain when the other color fades. Aquarium conditions seem to affect the colors of the males as at times it appears rather pale, often being mistaken for a female. But like turning on an electric light, some mysterious force goes to work and its breath-taking color comes back in an instant. A fascinating, changeable fish. Breeding is like "Barbs," already described. Best temperature, 80 degrees. Ideal aquarium fish, hardy, peaceful and easy to feed. Average size, 2 inches. *Nigrofasciatus* means "black-banded."

Barbus conchonius

Barbus lateristriga

Barbus oligolepis

Barbus everetti

Barbus sumatranus

BARBUS CONCHONIUS
ROSY BARB

THIS Barb is the hardiest of a hardy genus, found living quite well in outdoor pools during the summer and standing many ranges of temperature and thriving as a result. This is also one of the best-known Barbs, being ideal for the novice to experiment with because of its easy breeding habits. Breeds as other Barbs and is very prolific. Eats anything. Average size, 2½ inches. Body is metallic, suffused with a rosy hue. All fins are red with a darker color around the edge. The male shows more color and is slightly smaller than the female. Its fins are lighter and body color faint. Both fish have a round dark spot on the body near the tail. Always available, one of the most inexpensive of all the Barbs.

BARBUS LATERISTRIGA
T BARB

THE common name is apt for this Barb. Body is burnished silver. A dark line starts at the tail and advances through the body, where it meets a wide black band around the fish, thus forming a T behind gill plate. A smaller band is noticed that fades as the fish gets older. No bright colors adorn this Barb, but it provides a contrast in the community tank and has a very hardy, peaceful nature. Eats anything and breeds as other Barbs. Average size, 2½ inches. Grows to 5 inches. *Lateristriga* means "lateral stripes." Always available. Most Barbs, being prolific breeders, are out of the rare fish class and seldom have to be imported.

BARBUS TITTEYA
CHERRY BARB

THIS is an attractive Barb with a very dejected look. The body appears sunken, but this is a peculiarity of the species and not due to ill health. Naturally slow swimmers. They are gentle and live well with other fish. Body color is brown with a blue-black stripe from the eye to the tail. Undersides are light with reddish tinge, eye red with gold circle. All fins are cherry red, pronounced in the male, lighter in the female. A beautiful Barb, breeds as others of the genus, but must be watched or will eat the eggs soon after spawning. In these Barbs, one male is sufficient for breeding, as 2 may engage in a dispute that would ruin both of them for some time. Eats any type of food. Average size, 1½ inches. Best temperature, 70 to 80 degrees.

ESOMUS MALAYENSIS

FLYING BARB

THE common name of this Barb should intrigue the fancier not familiar with the species. The name is derived because of the wide pectoral fins that resemble wings. Its flying ability is not developed to any great extent, but since it is usually near the surface of the water it is well to have a cover on the aquarium, as they have been known to jump out of open tanks. The body has a very brilliant silvery sheen. It has a dark eye with gold circle and a spot in the tail that resembles the eye. Not colorful, but a strange, attractive fish that lends an odd touch to the community collection. Quite hardy and peaceful. Average size, 1½ inches. Likes Daphnia and all dried food. Breeds as other "Barbs" except for a slight peculiarity, the male pushes against the female to release the eggs. The female in turn pushes the male to aid in fertilization. An interesting process to observe. The young are delicate and hard to raise. Tempting food must be offered and temperature kept steady. Breeding temperature, 80 degrees. *Esomus* meaning "slender body," *malayensis* meaning "Malayan region."

RASBORA HETEROMORPHA

RASBORA

ALTHOUGH there are quite a few species of Rasbora, mention of that name immediately brings to mind the beautiful and popular "Queen of the Aquarium," the *heteromorpha*. For years in its royal dignity it repelled all efforts of scientific breeders and remained in the rare and expensive class. Then came spasmodic

reports from different sections of the country, the Rasbora had
at last been bred. While this was true, the spawns were not large
and only a very small percentage survived, and these were very
delicate and matured slowly. Since that time, breeders persisted
and duplicated former conditions, but still could not develop a
large enough supply for the commercial market.

Considering they come from far-off Asia, shipments are not apt
to be arriving for some time. However, we know breeders will
not give up until this fish can be bred in quantity. So we hope one
will make a lucky strike and produce enough *Heteromorpha* so
amateur breeders can get stock to try their hand at this fascinating
process that offers such a challenge.

To distinguish sex the only method considered sure is the gold
line above the blue-black wedge on the body. This is brilliant and
deep in the male. In the female it is light and only faintly dis-
cernible. Place the pair in an aquarium well planted with Cryptocoryne or Giant Sagittaria. Water temperature about 80 degrees.
They remain there for several days until the water ages just right.
The male swims over and around the female while female rubs
plants with underside in an upside-down position. The male catches
female like this and circles its body around female in an ardent
embrace until several eggs appear which are attached to the leaf.
This is repeated under other plants until 40 or 50 eggs are deposited
on different leaves. The process usually takes several hours. Parents
must then be removed to safeguard the eggs which hatch in about
24 hours. Fine infusoria may then be fed a little at a time.

The *Heteromorpha* is hardy, peaceful and eats any food offered.
Average size, one inch. A valuable fish, worthy of a place in any
aquarium with rare and beautiful fish.

RASBORA TRILINEATA

THE trilineata is seen from time to time, but has not been on the
market lately. It was received with open arms by rare fish collectors, who always want something new and different. Very
few have succeeded, to my knowledge, in developing many *Rasbora trilineata*, although recently several breeders have been more
successful.

The body is almost transparent with small yellow and black stripes on the tail. Not a flashy fish, but pretty as well as individual. Eats all types of food. Is hardy and peaceful and lives well with other fish. Average size, 1½ inches. *Trilineata* meaning with 3 lines.

RASBORA MEINKENI

THE *Meinkeni* was named for Herman Meinken, a German aquarist. Average size, 1½ inches. Hardy and peaceful. The body color is bright gold with brownish line from eye to tail. All fins are clear. The female is slightly larger with a full rounded body. The male is very slender. Temperature, 70 to 82 degrees.

RASBORA MACULATA

DWARF RASBORA

THIS tiny Rasbora has long been a favorite among the experienced fanciers. Averaging less than one inch, its sturdy body, erect fins and distinctive markings make it a fish to be desired by everyone. The body is salmon red with several blue-black spots. Fins are red tinged with a faint black edging on the dorsal and anal. Males have a very pronounced spot behind the gill that is very faint or absent in the female. Breeding has been accomplished to a very small degree by real experienced breeders. They report breeding habits as the *heteromorpha* without the embrace. The male fertilizes the eggs immediately. Young are minute and must be fed very fine food. Water for breeding must be well aged. Temperature about 80 degrees. Hardy for their size, the Maculata eat the smallest live foods and some dried food. Dainty and peaceful, they live well with other small fish. *Maculata* meaning spotted.

MELANOTAENIA NIGRANS

AUSTRALIAN RAINBOW FISH

FROM "Down Under" this beautiful and hardy fish, belonging to

Pair of *Rasbora heteromorpha*
Rasbora maculata
Rasbora taeniata
Melanotaenia nigrans

the Atherinidae family, has been introduced with great success into community tanks and also outdoor pools. An easy breeder, it spawns in pools or aquariums with no trouble and has become quite common. Breeding habits as for egg layers.

Brilliant colors are on the body in striped form with red and yellow predominating. Average size, 2 inches. Stands temperatures from 60 to 85 degrees and eats anything. Is peaceful, but likes a large aquarium to provide room for fast swimming. Very active.

CORYDORAS

SILURIDAE — CATFISH

The South American Catfish we use as scavengers in the aquarium are also interesting and likable fish. No tank really seems complete without one or 2 of these hard-working Corydoras scurrying around the bottom in search of some bit of food overlooked by other fish. They are peaceful and inoffensive, providing many laughs for the fancier with their comical, solemnlike appearance. In compiling our royalty of the aquarium, we cannot resist appointing these the Court Jesters. The ability to wink is among their many and varied accomplishments. They possess eyelids. The only species among tropicals with this added feature.

In breeding, all have the same general habits and are not considered too difficult to propagate. Females are larger than the male with rounded ventral fins. In the male these fins come to a point. Place a healthy, full-bodied pair in a 5-gallon tank, slightly alkaline water, temperature about 75 degrees. Plants suggested are Sagittaria and Vallisneria or others with wide, firm leaves. When the time for spawning nears the male will hover near the female, nudging it frequently on the back and sides. After this they embrace in very unique fashion. The male rolls over and the female places her body against the male, remaining this way for very short intervals. Upon freeing themselves, the female has several eggs between the ventral fins. These are adhesive and are stuck firmly on a plant leaf, where they remain. This process is repeated over a period of several hours. From 80 to 100 eggs are disposed of in this fashion. These hatch in 4 or 5 days and seem to provide for themselves pretty well until small live daphnia are introduced for them to feed on. This can be started after the second week. If daphnia is not available, fine dried food may be substituted. The Catfish are a rather large family. We list only the most popular and the varieties usually seen in community aquariums.

CORYDORAS LEOPARDUS

LEOPARD CATFISH

FOR 10 years this *Corydoras* has been considered very popular by fanciers. The quaint markings and lively nature won friends wherever it was displayed. Average size, 2 inches. Very hardy. Black spots dot the nose, body and tail of the *leopardus*. Several black stripes start halfway through the body and run to the base of the tail. Dorsal fin has large black spot. Extremely peaceful as others of this species and will not fight under any circumstances.

CORYDORAS PALEATUS

THIS *Corydoras* is the most popular. Average size, 2 inches. Hardy and modest. Body is olive with black splotches. All fins are marked with black dots. Lives long and peacefully in community aquariums and does a yeoman's job in keeping the tank bottom free of refuse.

CORYDORAS AENEUS

SINCE all *Corydoras* are armored Catfish, we do not apply this as a common name to the *aeneus*, although it has often been referred to as such. Probably because of its formidable appearance. The body is dark green with a reddish tint along the scales. All fins are large and erect with a green cast. They have been spawned frequently. These fish are noted as tireless workers, busying themselves day and night grubbing in the sand for that extra choice morsel. This suggests a prodigious appetite and adds to their desirability as scavengers. The *Corydoras* in general survive con-

Fresh Water Blow Fish

Corydoras aeneus
Corydoras paleattus

Corydoras melanistius
Corydoras leopardus

ditions that prove fatal to other fish. Chief among these are foul water and high temperatures. They breathe from the top as Labyrinth fish and interrupt their eternal grubbing to flash to the top of the water and glide back again. This action is performed very quickly and woe betide the slow fish who happens to come in contact with one of their sharp fins. Not a common occurrence, but known to have happened in crowded tanks. Average size of the *aeneus*, 2 inches.

CORYDORAS RABAUTI

THIS is one of the latest *Corydoras* to be imported, arriving in 1941, and after classification was named for the famous collector, Auguste Rabaut. Slightly smaller than the *aeneus*, this species averages 1½ inches. Breeding as Corydoras, but has not responded with very large spawns, keeping in the "rare" class and will not be available until further imports build up a supply for the market. Very pretty in appearance. Body color is bronze with reddish tints. Dark band on the back from the dorsal to the tail. Fins clear.

Other *Corydoras* popular with fanciers and seen from time to time are the *Corydoras punctatus*, *lineatus* and *hastatus* (Dwarf Catfish). All are hardy, peaceful and good scavengers.

LORICARIA PARVA

THIS is a rare and unsual Catfish not seen of late, but included in most full shipments from So. America. Its length of 3 inches starts with wide head and body, narrowing down to a long, very slender tail. A magnificent dorsal, almost transparent, stands out sharply against the gray body color, interspersed with black patches that blend so well with rockwork in the aquarium. Breeding has been accomplished by experienced men but to a very slight degree. This fish has a suctionlike mouth that permits it to stick to the sides of rock and glass sides of the tank. Likes algae but sits for long periods without moving. Fairly hardy and peaceful. Likes worms and daphnia. Temperature, 72 to 80 degrees.

Otocinclus arnoldi   Astrodoras asterifrons   Callichthys callichthys
Loricaria parva   Plecostomus commersoni

OTOCINCLUS ARNOLDI

SUCKER CATFISH

A DAINTY scavenger, unlike the comical armoured Catfish, the *Otocinclus* is a thorough worker, slow and methodical. It cleans the plants of algae leaf by leaf and no doubt enjoys its work. A suckerlike surface permits the *Otocinclus* to hang from the sides of the aquarium or stick on a leaf. This is advantageous during breeding time, as the female sticks to the underside of a Ludwigia leaf, seeming to hold it with the ventral fins. When female departs, an egg will be found. The male repeats the process and fertilizes the egg. This is repeated, always one egg to a leaf, until about 25 or 30 are laid. These hatch in several days and young are similar to other egg-laying progeny. The body, from the mouth to the dorsal, is rather wide and narrows down toward the tail. The color is dull gold with a dark line from the nose to the tail. A pleasant fish, popular with fanciers and ideal for community aquariums. Eats anything, likes algae. Temperature, 70 to 80 degrees. Average size, 1½ inches. From the Amazon.

PLECOSTOMUS COMMERSONI

THIS is another sucker-type Catfish. Clings to any part of the aquarium and even to large plants. Likes algae and has decidedly nocturnal habits. Suggested for aquariums containing large specimens, as the average size is 3 inches and gets much larger. Never bred to this writer's knowledge. Considered very rare and the small supply that came in with other imports was quickly snapped up by fanciers.

A strange, interesting fish. The *commersoni* has a sturdy body, peculiarly shaped and a large sail-type, spiny dorsal. The body is gray, dotted with brown spots set close together and extending to all fins. Eats any type food and does not bother fish. Likes clean water. Temperature, 70 to 80 degrees.

CRYPTOPTERUS BICIRRHIS

GLASS CATFISH

THIS is a shimmering rarity from the Far East that does nothing to earn its keep in the aquarium except add a unique touch. Usually from 2 to 3 inches. The long, thin, transparent body shows the spine and fine bones with astounding clarity. The only touch of color is a silvery sac just behind the eye that contains the delicate mechanism that sustains life in the fish. Microscopic organs of digestion must do their work well as the Glass Catfish eats daphnia and worms shyly but with relish. Never bred. Imports from the Far East show a low mortality rate, so we must consider this fish fairly hardy. Best temperature, 75 degrees. Seen to best advantage against a thickly planted, green background. The name *bicirrhis* means "whiskers." Two project out from this oddity's nose.

Cryptopterus bicirrhus

The following will be devoted to miscellaneous fishes that are part of aquarium life. Some are peaceful. Others are not, but have some individual characteristics that make fanciers keep them alone or in company with others of their kind for decorative and unusual purposes.

TOXOTES JACULATOR

ARCHER FISH

THIS is a colorful native of the East Indies, a hunter that unseen approaches his prey. With deadly accuracy he looses his darts upon the unsuspecting victim, causing it to fall, where our sharp-shooter quickly snaps it up to provide an added tidbit in his diet. This dramatic build-up serves to introduce a sterling show fish, who never gives a performance without getting paid for it — none other than the *Toxotes jaculator* or ARCHER FISH. Discussed and drawn for a cartoon by Robert (Believe it or not) Ripley and referred to by lecturers on tropical fish whenever a speech lags for want of an unusual feature. The author, in talks before Aquarium Societies, includes this fish and receives satisfaction in having a truly interesting subject for discussion. In native surroundings, as in the aquarium, the Archer Fish is a top swimmer, always alert for a fly or bug to come within range of its watery pellets. Some years ago, in the wholesale aquarium where I worked, we had a splendid specimen in a large tank half full of water. To show a doubting customer that stories of the fish were true, I threw a roach in the water at the other end of the tank. This immediately made for the side and started to climb the glass sides. The Archer arrived at this time and up went the water from its mouth. A bull's-eye! Knocking the roach back in the water, with an easy motion the Archer dispatched it and circled looking for more. My customer, a mid-western dealer, bought the fish on the spot. No temperamental performer, the Archer fish will work if someone provides the material for its little act. Between performances, live food such as daphnia and worms are taken readily. Body is lemon-colored with wide dark bars on the sides. All fins are black. A distinctive fish, rare and valuable. Best water temperature, 75 degrees. Never been bred. Sex characteristics and breeding habits unknown. Seen from 3 to 5 inches.

Toxotes jaculator
Notopterus notopterus
Carapus fasciatus
Sternarchus schotti

ACANTHOPHTHALMUS KUHLI

THIS is a rare little loach, always in demand, but not seen for some time. Breeding habits unknown, although reports say it has been bred at least once in an aquarium. Its odd appearance and color make it a noval addition to the rare collection. Average size is 2 to 3 inches. The body is long and round like a snake, eel or worm. It is nocturnal and likes a soft bottom. Like the Catfish, it is con-

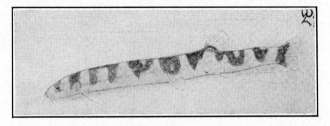

Acanthophthalmus kuhli

sidered a scavenger, but to a lesser degree. Roots around the bottom for bits of uneaten food. The body color is orange with about a dozen black patches along the back. Barbels are small and bushy like a miniature walrus. Easily fed, very hardy. From the Malay region. Best water temperature, 70 to 80 degrees.

BOTIA MACRACANTHUS

CLOWN LOACH

A VERY rare loach, expensive and usually snapped up by large Public Aquariums in New York, Chicago, Boston and Philadelphia. A show fish with dazzling colors. It eats any type of food and is also considered a scavenger. Breeding has failed thus far, but it would be a triumph, indeed, if it were accomplished. Body color is burnt orange with reddish tinge, 3 blue-black bands around the body, one very narrow around the head passing through the eye. The fins and nose are a brilliant red. The well-shaped tail is also red. The Clown Loach has a disconcerting habit of laying over on its side and playing "dead." This caused some fanciers deep concern until it was learned that this position was a favorite with the fish and was often practiced as means of getting a good rest. Length, 2 to 3 inches. Hardy. Temperature, 70 to 80 degrees. Habitat, Borneo.

APHYOSEMION AUSTRALE

LYRETAIL OR CAMERONENSIS

THE males of this species are of exquisite beauty, as may be seen from the illustration. The females have neither this color nor the elaborate fins, merely being used for propagation. This is fairly easy. Place a pair in a small tank of about 2 or 3 gallons' capacity. Temperature, 76 to 78 degrees. Plants producing the best results are *Riccia* and *Utricularia minor*. Allow these to float on the surface. The fish spawn and deposit the eggs on the plant mats, which may be removed completely and placed in smaller containers. Always replace plant mats with new ones as the fish, once started, spawn quite regularly (every 10 days or so). Each batch of eggs contain 15 to 25 young when hatched. This takes from 10 to 12 days. After this occurs, feed minute quantities of very fine food or infusoria until size allows them larger foods. In properly kept acquariums, the Lyretail has proved to be quite hardy. Eats anything but prefers live food. Is peaceful and lives well with other fish. Average size, 2 inches. Originally from Cape Lopez, So. Africa, and formerly called the Cape Lopez. A beautiful and prolific fish.

PANCHAX CHAPERI

THIS is one of the most popular of the Panchax group. The *chaperi* has lived in community tanks and gotten along very well with the other fish. It is hardy, prolific and very colorful, as may be seen from the illustration. A definite sex distinction is the red patch at the throat of the male and a point at the end of the tail. A good fish for the novice fancier to breed and display. Breeding and keeping as described. Average size, 2 inches. Habitat, the Gold Coast of Africa.

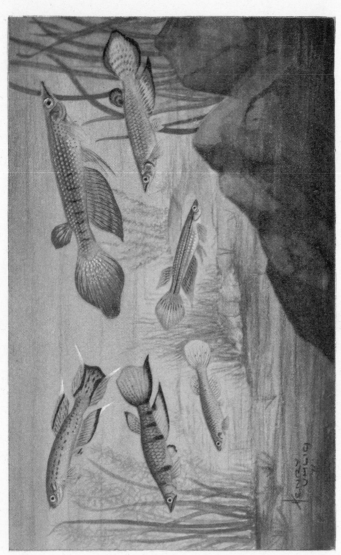

Aphyosemion australe (Male)   *Panchax lineatus*
Panchax chaperi *Panchax parvus* *Panchax panchax*
Aphyosemion australe (Female)

PANCHAX PARVUS

This is a small popular *Panchax*, averaging 1½ inches in size. Although not as colorful as the others in this group, still it has a modest beauty and peaceful nature that makes fanciers include them in community collections. Sex may be determined by the anal and dorsal fins. The males are well developed, coming to a point. The female has rounded fins and fainter color. The male in the illustration has green on the top half of the body fading to light pink below. Red and gold spots dot the sides, fins are orange tinged with red.

A prolific breeder. As in all *Panchax*, parents should be removed when spawning is complete. The young mature rapidly when fed properly. The *Panchax* are sluggish fish in the aquarium, but the *parvus* is the most active of all. Good eaters, they thrive on live food. Best temperature, 70 to 80 degrees. This *Panchax* is from India originally, but has not been imported for some time.

PANCHAX PANCHAX

All Panchax varieties must be watched in the aquarium. They are naturally pugnacious and are apt to nip smaller fish. Therefore, if kept community, keep with larger types. This variety has quite a color range, but the illustration seems to have captured the average fish. It can be recognized as *Panchax panchax*. Average size, 2 inches. Very hardy. Habitat India. Best temperature, 75 to 80 degrees. Eats anything. Likes live food. Breeding similar to Lyretail.

PANCHAX LINEATUS

This is one of the confirmed fin nippers and is not for community tanks; usually larger than the average *Panchax* (3 inches). It is nevertheless popular for its beauty (see illustration) and easy breeding habits (as described). Many fanciers keep several varieties of Panchax together for show and to breed. However, Lineatus males have often injured the females and must be watched at all times during spawning. Keeping as *Panchax panchax*. Panchax is the native name. *Lineatus* means striped. Habitat, India.

RIVULUS UROPHTHALMUS
RED RIVULUS

THIS genus, like the *Panchax*, are very sluggish in their motions and pugnacious toward other fish. They are kept in community aquariums, but must be watched for signs of fin nipping. The Red or Golden Rivulus, as it is frequently called, is vividly colored, usually golden orange on the body. Rows of red dots are neatly arranged on the sides, much more brilliant in the male. This fish is considered a "sport." The real *urophthalmus* being green with faint red spots and a spot at the base of the tail. In breeding both fish are prolific and good for beginners to start out on. Parents will eat eggs and young if allowed to remain after spawning. Habits are similar to *Panchax*. A cover should be provided for aquarium, as these fish jump quite high out of the water if disturbed. Average size, 2 inches. Temperature, 75 to 80 degrees. Likes live food but will eat dried food if not fed too often.

RIVULUS CYLINDRACEOUS
GREEN RIVULUS

THE hardy and prolific nature of the *cylindraceous* is known to most fanciers. For this reason it has managed to keep its popularity. In community aquariums it has been very peaceful towards all fish, even smaller types. Colors in the male are nicely blended and the green body has a yellowish cast that affords a background for the haphazard blue-and-red spots that dot the sides, anal and ventral fins faintly red. Caudal fin has bluish cast. The female is less striking and easily identified by the characteristic spot all females of this genus display at the base of the tail. Length, 2 inches. Likes live food. Temperature, 70 to 75 degrees. *Rivulus* meaning "river" or "rivulet." *Cylindraceous* means cylindrical in shape. Habitat is Cuba.

AMBASSIS LALA
GLASS FISH

THE *Ambassis lala* is another fish of the rare class in this country and is often seen in aquariums with delicate and expensive fish.

Frequently imported, the *lala* survived long journeys that proved, in spite of its dainty, fragile appearance, it could take it when the going was tough.

A difficult fish to breed, but perseverance will result in success. It is advisable to have 2 males to a female. Use a large tank (15 gallons), supply floating plants and aged water, temperature about 80 degrees. Males are colorful and are easily distinguished from the faintly marked female. The eggs are sprayed into plant mats while the fish are together. These are tiny and very hard to see. When spawning is complete, remove parents as a precaution, even though they have been allowed to remain in other tanks successfully. The eggs hatch in from 8 to 10 hours. Very fine infusoria is needed to feed the young.

The male *Ambassis lala* is a striking picture in the aquarium. Its tiny body looks larger because of its erect fins. The body is transparent like glass. The spine and bones are seen clearly as in *Cryptopterus bicirrhis*. The silver sac is noted, but body has blue and red iridescence. The dorsal and anal fins are tipped with blue, the anal with red and blue edging. Average size, 1½ inches. India is their habitat and it is reported they are quite common there. Will eat some dried food, but prefers finely chopped worms and daphnia.

PANTODON BUCHHOLZI

BUTTERFLY FISH

THIS unique fish from Africa has large, well-developed pectoral fins, shaped like wings, used to skim along the surface of the water in their native surroundings. This, however, does not prevent them from being kept in an aquarium by themselves. They are not recommended for community tanks, as they have jaws that open very wide on demand and could swallow a fish with ease. They favor live food. I remember one large shipment that came in and was put in a large aquarium. Experiments were started in feeding and it developed that roaches and flies were their favorite diet. We set traps and caught many and it was really a sight to see them swoop through the water and grab their prey all in one motion. We found out later that their fondness for these roaches was started aboard ship. The caretaker, needing live food, sup-

Pantodon buchholzi
Ambassis lala
Ambassis commersoni
Luciocephalus pulcher

plied what was handy to their evident satisfaction. I've seen these fish catch large diving beetles and water scorpions in their powerful jaws and in two bits they were gone. Breeding is very difficult, but has been accomplished. The females have short wings, full bodies and rounded fins. The young require exacting care. A cover must be kept on the aquarium constantly, as these fish are surface swimmers and are noted for their jumping ability. A real fresh water flying fish. Average size, 5 inches. All fins and tail are long and flowing. Body very sturdy. Long, powerful jaws and large eyes that always seem to have a baleful glare. They will eat dried daphnia, meal and earthworms, baby fish or raw lean beef. Temperature, 72 to 78 degrees.

MONOCIRRHUS POLYACANTHUS

LEAF FISH

PICTURE a dried leaf floating silently downstream and you have a perfect description of the So. American Leaf Fish. This is a strange and unusual aquarium fish, definitely not peaceful, as small fish disappear very fast when the "Leaf" gets around. Their mouths open very wide and the male is easily identified by the tiny stem

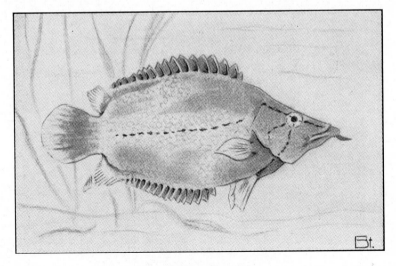

Monocirrhus polyacanthus

protruding from its lower lip. The female does not have this appendage. Colors provide perfect camouflage for this fish. Its collectors tell me they often pass them by. Only by seeing them move can they be sure they are really fish and not leaves. Brown, rusty red, dull yellow and grayish black all blend in perfect schemes to protect the Leaf Fish from its enemies. It is interesting to watch the casual way it hangs in the aquarium near the top, remaining that way for hours. As soon as a fish is introduced, be it the fast Zebra or innocent Guppy, chain lightning is released and the luckless fish never knew just what happened. This can be repeated a dozen times or more. The Leaf Fish will literally eat himself to death. Average size, 2½ inches. Temperature, 75 to 80 degrees.

Breeding is difficult, usually at 80 degrees. Somewhat like the Cichlids. Parents will eat eggs and young if left in breeding tank. All Leaf Fish swim with head down in the water.

GYMNOTUS CARAPO
KNIFE FISH

THESE are strange, pugnacious fish that are for show only. The common name aptly describes the thin, bladelike body that is capable of swimming forward and backward with no stops in between. Trying to net this fish is a trying job as they go into reverse with amazing speed. Breeding habits are unknown and are likely to remain so. Not enough are imported as in native haunts they attain a length of 12 inches. Average aquarium size is 5 inches, but these continue to grow. Body is dark brown, long and flat, with yellowish stripes from head to pointed tail. All fins, with the exception of the anal and pectoral, are missing. The anal fin is long and rippling. Very hardy; temperature range, 60 to 80 degrees. Must be fed live food, will take bits of raw meat. A South American oddity.

TETRODON FLUVIATILIS
TETRODON CUTCUTIA
BLOWFISH OR PUFFERS

THESE are brackish water fishes that cannot remain in entirely fresh water for very long without showing distress signals. They are very active in the aquarium and provide quite a show for the spectators. They have the unique ability of being able to blow themselves up like a balloon when startled, also when held in the hand and the belly is rubbed or tickled. When placed back in the water the air rushes out and they sink to the bottom. Then they resume their swimming, none the worse for their experience. Fanciers have kept several together in well-aerated aquariums containing fresh and sea water. They live happily eating live food such as earthworms, small snails and daphnia. Not to be kept with other fish as they are aggressive, preferring their own kind. The *fluviatilis* has a dark green body with a white belly, green patches on the back covered with black dots. Cutcuttia have a light olive green back with dark stripes across, white spots all over. Belly pure white.

Neither fish has been bred. Imported from India. Temperature, 70 to 80 degrees. Length, 3 to 4 inches.

SCATOPHAGUS ARGUS
SCAT

From the Indian and Pacific Oceans we receive this brilliantly colored fish. Lives in brackish water and aquariums that are well aerated. Will eat anything, even dried food, and likes a leaf of lettuce occasionally. The body is flat shape with prominent erect fins. The ground color is metallic green with black spots. Red and orange are seen at various points from the nose to the tail. This is the average 1½-inch aquarium size. Larger 5-inch specimens are not so brightly colored. No breeding information is available, but can be kept with other fish as the Scats are known as peaceful, amusing pets in the aquarium. Temperature, 72 to 77 degrees. Not available now but offered from time to time.

MONADACTYLUS ARGENTEUS

The *Monodactylus* in shape resembles the *scalare*, but does not have the long flowing fins. The body color is silvery with a blue sheen. Two black lines across the front part of the fish, one running through the eye. The dorsal is a golden yellow with deep edging, tail and lower fins have a yellow sheen. The *Monodactylus* originate in salt water streams, but have been successfully kept in fresh water community aquariums. Not only did they thrive, but they grew several inches in size. They make the change from fresh water to salt water and show no ill effects. Once acclimated to pure salt water, it is not advisable to try them in fresh water again. This may have disastrous effects. It is a very pretty, active fish, friendly and hardy. Average size, 3 inches, but grows fairly well in aquariums and can reach 6 inches. Likes live food. Best temperature, 70 to 77 degrees. Never been bred and not available at the present time, but a fish we hope to see soon.

BRACHYGOBIUS XANTHAZONA

BUMBLE BEE FISH

THIS has always been a popular fish with fanciers that lean toward the unusual in their aquariums. Of late stocks have dwindled and it is seldom seen on the market. But it appears often enough to allow rabid fanciers the opportunity of obtaining a pair for their community collections.

Several authorities accuse this fish of being pugnacious and nipping fins of the other specimens in the tank. My answer to this charge is that the *"Gobius"* is a very inactive fish, likes to perch on rocks or plants and does not look for trouble. Therefore, trouble has to come to him and he is capable of protecting himself at all times. In my own tank a pair of Bumble Bee Fish lived amiably with other fish for over a year. I finally gave them to a friend who lost them soon after by a freak accident.

The Bumble Bees can be bred, but care and patience are required to make this successful. They like very old still water and are considered fairly hardy. The average size is 1½ inches. They eat all types of food but prefer worms and daphnia.

The resemblance to a Bumble Bee is quite marked. The body color is yellow with wide black bands circling fish from mouth to tail. Best temperature, 75 degrees. From the Malay Peninsula, but bred in Europe in quantities and shipped here until present conditions made this impossible.

Monodactylus argenteus
Scatophagus argus
Scatophagus rubrifrons
Scatophagus multifasciatum

PTEROIS VOLITANS L.

THIS satanic-looking, salt-water fish inhabits the Indian Ocean. Large Public Aquariums are constantly begging importers to get them a specimen at any price!

The ferocious glare of this spiny, Zebra-striped Lion Fish fascinates spectators to a marked degree. When they learn of the subtle poison it carries, interest is more intense.

Because of this poison, concentrated in the spiny dorsal fin, the *Pterois volitans* is known as one of the most dangerous and difficult fish to collect and transport. To illustrate the strange, mysterious power of the fish, there is the story of an experienced collector, expert in his line, who was transferring this fish from an aquarium to a shipping tank. A careless move resulted in his being stung by the creature. In a matter of seconds he fell to the floor unconscious. A Chinese doctor was called, and, since the symptoms indicated a Cobra bite, the patient was treated accordingly. The doctor worked diligently for eight hours before he was able to revive the collector, who suffered drowsiness and weak eyes for 2 days after the incident. Extreme care must be exercised in handling this fish. The average reader will never come in contact with it, but other readers, who specialize in rare and exotic fish, may at some time profit by the knowledge that silent death lurks in a mere sting of the grotesque dorsal fin.

LION FISH

INDEX

INDEX (Cont.)

INDEX (Cont.)

Press of

INNES & SONS
Phila., Pa.